RICHARD DARLINGTON

Borgo Press Books Written or Translated by FRANK J. MORLOCK

Anna Karenina: A Play in Five Acts, by Edmond Guiraud, from the Novel by Leo Tolstoy

Anthony: A Play in Five Acts, by Alexandre Dumas, Père

The Children of Captain Grant: A Play in Five Acts, by Jules Verne and Adolphe d'Ennery

Crime and Punishment: A Play in Three Acts, by Frank J. Morlock, from the Novel by Fyodor Dostoyevsky

Falstaff: A Play in Four Acts, by William Shakespeare, John Dennis, William Kendrick, and Frank J. Morlock

Jesus of Nazareth: A Play in Three Acts, by Paul Demasy

Joan of Arc: A Play in Five Acts, by Charles Desnoyer

The Lily of the Valley: A Play in Five Acts, by Théodore Barrière and Arthur de Beauplan, from the Novel by Honoré de Balzac

Michael Strogoff: A Play in Five Acts, by Adolphe d'Ennery and Jules Verne

The Mysteries of Paris: A Play in Five Acts, by Eugène Sue and Prosper Dinaux

Peau de Chagrin: A Play in Five Acts, by Louis Judicis, from the Novel by Honoré de Balzac

A Raw Youth: A Play in Five Acts, by Frank J. Morlock, from the Novel by Fyodor Dostoyevsky

Richard Darlington: A Play in Three Acts, by Alexandre Dumas, Père, and Prosper Dinaux

The San Felice: A Play in Five Acts, by Maurice Drack, from the Novel by Alexander Dumas, Père

Shylock, the Merchant of Venice: A Play in Three Acts, by Alfred de Vigny

The Voyage Through the Impossible: A Play in Three Acts, by Jules Verne and Adolphe d'Ennery

William Shakespeare: A Play in Six Acts, by Ferdinand Dugué

RICHARD DARLINGTON

A Play in Three Acts

by

Alexandre Dumas, Père
& Prosper Dinaux

Translated and Adapted by Frank J. Morlock

The Borgo Press

An Imprint of Wildside Press LLC

MMIX

Copyright © 2001, 2009 by Frank J. Morlock

All rights reserved. No part of this book may be reproduced without the expressed written consent of the author. Professionals are warned that this material, being fully protected under the copyright laws of the United States of America, and all other countries of the Berne and Universal Copyright Convention, is subject to a royalty. All rights, including all forms of performance now existing or later invented, but not limited to professional, amateur, recording, motion picture, recitation, public reading, radio, television broadcasting, DVD, and Role Playing Games, and all rights of translation into foreign languages, are expressly reserved. Particular emphasis is placed on the question of readings, and all uses of these plays by educational institutions, permission for which must be secured in advance from the author's publisher, Wildside Press, 9710 Traville Gateway Dr. #234, Rockville, MD 20850 (phone 301-762-1305). Printed in the United States of America

www.wildsidebooks.com

FIRST WILDSIDE EDITION

CONTENTS

Cast of Characters 7

Prologue 9

Act I, Scene 1 34
Act I, Scene 2 67
Act II, Scene 3 85
Act II, Scene 4 107
Act II, Scene 5 121
Act III, Scene 6 131
Act III, Scene 7 154
Act III, Scene 8 159

About the Author 171

DEDICATION

To Milan Jurecka

CAST OF CHARACTERS

Richard Darlington
Robertson Fildy, under the name Mawbray
Thompson
The Marquis Da Silva
Doctor Grey
A Stranger (Unknown)
Sir Stansen
The First Lord of the Treasury
The Secretary of State for the Interior
The Secretary of State for the Department of War
The High Bailiff
Outram
A Constable
First Citizen
Second Citizen
An Usher
A Yellow Elector, a servant of Derby's
A Servant
Blackfort
A Blue Elector
Jenny, Doctor Grey's daughter
Caroline De Silva
Mistress Grey
Betty
Miss Wilmer
A Merchant of Blue Ribbons
A Merchant of Yellow Ribbons
Electors, Commissars, People, Servants, Children, etc.

PROLOGUE

The House of the Doctor.

The office of Doctor Grey, shelves filled with books, a window to the left. Door at the back and doors on each side.

At rise, Doctor Grey is seated at a table with a lamp on it—his wife is standing near him with her hand resting on his shoulder while with her other hand she holds a candle.

DOCTOR
Goodnight, Anna—I won't delay joining you.

MRS. GREY
Yes, you tell me that, and then you spend half the night working, and tomorrow, hardly will it be day when they come to find you for some patient. Think that you are the only doctor in this village and that if you fall ill who will care for you?

DOCTOR
Goodnight, Anna.

MRS. GREY
That means I'm boring you, right? Look, do you need anything before I go?

DOCTOR
Nothing—fine.

MRS. GREY
(putting on his green glasses) At least put on your green glasses they'll protect your sight— Will you promise me to keep them on? Yes? Goodnight—don't work too late—especially.

(she leaves)

DOCTOR
No, no—don't worry only an hour more—

(He goes to his library and pulls out two or three volumes to read— The noise of a carriage coming at a gallop can be heard from the street.)

ROBERTSON
(outside) Postilion! Postilion!

POSTILION
(stopping the carriage) Hey!

ROBERTSON
Get down and rap on that window where that light is.

POSTILION
Yes, master.

DOCTOR
That's here.

POSTILION
(rapping) Ho! Hola!

DOCTOR
(opening the window) What is it, my brave lad?

ROBERTSON
Sir, is there a doctor in the village?

DOCTOR
Yes.

ROBERTSON
Good?

DOCTOR
I'd be a biased judge, sir—I am, yes.

ROBERTSON
You are the only one?

DOCTOR
Yes, sir.

ROBERTSON
Be good enough to open the door for me.

DOCTOR
I'll go call—

WOMAN'S VOICE
Oh, no, no—sir—don't call anyone. Open yourself.

DOCTOR
I'm on my way.

(opens the door and recoils)

A masked man—what do you want from me?

ROBERTSON
Silence—and fear nothing.

DOCTOR
Still, sir—

ROBERTSON
Doctor, isn't your profession to help those who are ill?

DOCTOR
It's more than my profession, it's my duty.

ROBERTSON
Then such help is urgent when all delay would lead to the death of one of God's creatures—To save her do you need to know her name or see her face?

DOCTOR
No, sir.

ROBERTSON
Well, there's a woman in that carriage, a woman who is ill, who needs you—who will die if you don't bring her help—momentarily even.

DOCTOR
But can't I know to whom—?

ROBERTSON
I repeat, sir, hardly ten minutes remains to you—and I would need more than an hour to give you explanations which I swear to you that you would take no interest in, so personal are they to me.

DOCTOR
I am ready.

ROBERTSON
One question more, sir—if this woman cannot leave as soon as she has received your attention—will you consent in the name of humanity to hide her in your home from all eyes—If I swear to you on honor no political cause forces us to surround ourselves in this mystery?

DOCTOR
Yes, sir, I will do it.

ROBERTSON
Are you married, doctor?

DOCTOR
What's that question for?

ROBERTSON
(taking his hand) To know if your wife is as excellent a woman as you are a brave man—

DOCTOR
I believe so.

ROBERTSON
Well, be so good as to call her, I beg you—Her help will be necessary—The person who demands help is of her sex.

DOCTOR
I am going to do it.

ROBERTSON
Thanks!

(placing a purse on the table)

Not to be quits with you—all the gold of King George would not suffice for that—but to indemnify you, to the extent it is in my power, at least, for the inconvenience I am causing.

POSTILION
(at the door) The young lady is calling you, sir.

ROBERTSON
I'm here—I'm here.

(goes out)

DOCTOR
(knocking at his wife's door) Anna! Anna!

MRS. GREY
(in her room)
What's all this racket?

DOCTOR
Some travelers who need both our help. So come quickly, since you haven't gone to bed.

(Mrs. Grey enters as Robertson carries in the young woman and places her on a chaise-longue.)

MRS. GREY
(terrified by Robertson's mask) Oh—see that!

DOCTOR
Silence!

ROBERTSON
(to Caroline) Are you still hurting, my angel?

CAROLINE
Oh, yes, much—much.

ROBERTSON
Doctor.

DOCTOR
(going to Caroline and taking her pulse) Sir, this young woman is on the point of giving birth.

ROBERTSON
And we mustn't think of going much further, right?

DOCTOR
Impossible!

CAROLINE
(to Mrs. Grey) You will take care of me, Madame?

MRS. GREY
(taking her hand) Like my sister.

CAROLINE
Oh, how good you are.

(leaning her head on Mrs. Grey's arms)

I am hurting indeed.

DOCTOR
Anna, give your room to Madame, and go prepare it. Hurry.

MRS. GREY
Should I waken Alix?

ROBERTSON
Who is Alix?

DOCTOR
Our serving girl—but she has the fault of being a little talkative and that wouldn't be convenient for us, would it?

ROBERTSON
Oh! No, no—Madame, you will have more trouble, but we must owe you our life the more.

CAROLINE
And God will reward you, Mistress.

(Mrs. Grey goes out)

ROBERTSON
Caroline, I am going to order the Postilion to place your bags and trunks here.

CAROLINE
Oh, no, no, don't leave me; I tremble if you leave me for an instant.

ROBERTSON
Doctor, would you have the goodness? A thousand pardons.

DOCTOR
(going to the door) Why, without a doubt.

CAROLINE
They seem like worthy people.

ROBERTSON
Yes, yes, but what a curse—not six leagues further to the seaport where everything was prepared for our flight, and we find ourselves here in this wretched little burg—where we shall find neither the care nor the necessary talent. Oh! We are indeed wretched.

CAROLINE
I am suffering less, Robertson, I am suffering less.

ROBERTSON
You are suffering less? Well, perhaps we could start again?

CAROLINE
Oh, no,—but here—can you take off your mask?

ROBERTSON
Far away as this village is, the Doctor might have been there and seen me.

CAROLINE
You were really well known in London?

ROBERTSON
Yes, yes—let's talk about something else.

CAROLINE
Yes—let's talk about my father.

ROBERTSON
(stamping his foot) Your father!

CAROLINE
You judge him ill.

ROBERTSON
As all men do.

CAROLINE
He loves me.

ROBERTSON
Less than he loves his name.

CAROLINE
If you had allowed me to tell him?

ROBERTSON
He would have forbidden you to see me.

CAROLINE
Why?

ROBERTSON
He is of the nobility and I am a commoner.

CAROLINE
But when he learned—

ROBERTSON
What?

CAROLINE
That you have saved my life.

ROBERTSON
What's that?

CAROLINE
At the risk of yours.

ROBERTSON
Every boatman on the Thames does that everyday now; do they ask in marriage the young girls they save.

CAROLINE
But you aren't a boatman are you?

ROBERTSON
Would to heaven I were!

CAROLINE
Oh—he would have been mollified.

ROBERTSON
Yes, and in his mollification, he would have had one of his valets throw me a purse. If I am not noble, at least I am rich and I have no need of his gold.

CAROLINE
Oh, Robertson, Robertson, I am hurting.

ROBERTSON
Doctor!

DOCTOR
(returning and going to Mrs. Grey's room) Right away.

CAROLINE
And if my father is pursuing us?

ROBERTSON
That's what torments me!

CAROLINE
Oh, if I were to see him again, before becoming your wife—Robertson I would die of shame.

ROBERTSON
Ah—there you are, doctor.

DOCTOR
(returning from his wife's room) Everything is ready.

(Caroline holds Robertson by the hand.)

ROBERTSON
Listen darling—I've got to hide the carriage, un-yoke the horses—if by chance your father took the same road as we, this equipage could betray us—listen—

(A carriage passes by at a high speed)

(Robertson goes to the door)

Listen! You can't see a thing—it's as black as a night in hell out there! I'll return right away. Courage, my Caroline! I will be right back.

CAROLINE
Oh, come back quickly—I will die if you are not here—

(She goes into the room. Robertson leaves and Mrs. Grey remains alone on stage)

MRS. GREY
He's some great Lord—why does he still keep his mask on? He seems to really love his wife. Poor little thing, may she be happier than I, and keep the child God has given her! She mustn't know one of the greatest sorrows in this world.

ROBERTSON
(returning) Mistress, what's your name, if you please—? Mistress?

MRS. GREY
Anna Grey.

ROBERTSON
Mistress Grey, I've hardly had time to speak to your husband. I was going to do it when the condition of my wife demanded his attention, but like him, Mistress, you have a face that commands confidence and I am going to share mine with you.

MRS. GREY
Speak, sir.

ROBERTSON
From motives that are no interest to you—I am forced to keep my face hidden—don't be worried about this mask—it covers the face of an honorable man.

MRS. GREY
I believe it, sir—

ROBERTSON
Let it suffice you to know, Madame, that the happiness of two lives would be completely compromised if I were recognized and I say this to you, Mistress, because one of two things is going to happen—Either we will be forced to leave as soon as the accouchement is over.

MRS. GREY
But that would risk killing that young woman.

ROBERTSON
So, it's the last probable of two hypotheses—or, alternatively, we will remain here until her recovery.

MRS. GREY
Oh—that would be better; a thousand times better.

ROBERTSON
I will try that it be that way—but in any case, Mistress, I desire that you would be guided by this truth, in either case—The least indiscretion,—the least, could cause the ruin of three people the child who is going to see the light of day in any moment would be included innocent as he is of my sins,—assuming I had committed some,—in the sentence of banishment which strikes us.

MRS. GREY
Be perfectly easy on that account, sir.

ROBERTSON
It might still be better—if we were to leave now—

(trembling) Oh—is that a shout from Caroline?

MRS. GREY
Fear nothing. My husband won't leave her.

ROBERTSON
And your husband is skilled, right?

MRS. GREY
Don't worry—but go to her—and then later, much later you will tell me—

ROBERTSON
Me—go near her—! Near her when she's suffering—oh, I couldn't possibly see Caroline—suffer—that angel—What was I saying to you, Mistress?

MRS. GREY
You were speaking of your child.

ROBERTSON
Yes, I was saying it if were possible, if we could leave now, or even if we stayed fifteen days—that the health of our child won't permit us to take him. So, Mistress, I want to confide him to you as a second mother— Would you care for and pity a poor abandoned child? And four times a year—until the day I am permitted to come take him from you—you will receive a purse like this—Will it be enough?

MRS. GREY
It's a great deal—much too much but, all the same, sir, the surplus we will carefully preserve and if one day by some accident, which please God it won't,—he is deprived of his parents, he will find this little sum—And as for me—I've lost two children already—I'll become his mother.

ROBERTSON
My good Madame Grey! Oh—hear him—do you hear him?

MRS. GREY
Reassure yourself. And if this child remains with us, would it be indiscreet to ask you the name he should bear?

ROBERTSON
If it's a boy, Richard; if it's a girl, Caroline.

MRS. GREY
Those are only first names.

ROBERTSON
What's the name of this village?

MRS. GREY
Darlington.

ROBERTSON
Well, Richard, or Caroline Darlington—It's fitting that he take the family name of the village where he will have found a family.

(the noise of moaning)

Oh, Mistress, Mistress—Tell me again there is no danger! That child, that angel owes all her troubles to me. To come to me, she descended from such a height. Rank, fortune, family—She sacrificed all for me. Oh, I beg you, I supplicate you—help her—go be with her.

MRS. GREY
Why come there yourself.

ROBERTSON
Me, me—I would go mad! Oh, Madame Grey—In the name of heaven, I will stay alone—Go, go!

(Mrs. Gray leaves. Robertson falls to his knees) Oh—I didn't dare pray in front of someone! My God! My God! Take pity on us.

(rising) No more. If she dies, my God—! Without my being there to receive her last sigh—! Oh, I have to go there—I can't stand this uncertainty.

CAROLINE
(from the room) Robertson! Robertson!

ROBERTSON
(recoiling) Ah!

DOCTOR
(coming on stage) Where is he? Where is he?

ROBERTSON
Well?

DOCTOR
Well—bravo, bravo! A big boy—

ROBERTSON
(embracing him) You are our savior, our father! Oh—let me weep.

(he bursts into tears)

DOCTOR
Why, go hug your wife, your son.

ROBERTSON
Oh, I am crazy! Lead me there, I can't see what I am doing anymore, doctor.

DOCTOR
(pushing him into the room) This way, go on, go on—

(knocking at the street door)

(the doctor stops) What's that?

(More knocking.)

DOCTOR
What do you want?

Da SILVA
(in the street) In the name of the King! Open—or we'll break down the door!

DOCTOR
Who are you?

ANOTHER VOICE
The Constable. You must recognize my voice, Doctor—open to spare yourself trouble.

Da SILVA
Mr. Constable—don't be so polite—break down the door.

DOCTOR
(opening) Stop, gentlemen!

Da SILVA
(rushing in) Doctor Grey.

DOCTOR
That's me, sir.

Da SILVA
You will answer to me for the two of them, for they are in your home.

DOCTOR
Ho—don't push me too far—You are in my home, sir—Don't force me to remind you of it.

Da SILVA
Then answer!

DOCTOR
First of all, show me you have the right to question me.

Da SILVA
These gentlemen are the bearers of a warrant.

DOCTOR
Well, I will answer to these gentlemen if they justify themselves to me and not to you—by your accent it appears to me you are not even English.

Da SILVA
So be it—but take care. We know they are here, we followed them closer than they thought—They relayed at the last post—They haven't been seen at this one and in passing, I thought I recognized—I did recognize the carriage at your door—So think carefully—It would be useless and perhaps dangerous to lie.

DOCTOR
I never lie, sir.

Da SILVA
(throwing himself in a chair) Constable—do your duty.

CONSTABLE
Doctor Grey—did you receive a masked man in your home, sir?

DOCTOR
Yes, sir.

CONSTABLE
He was accompanied by a young woman.

DOCTOR
That's true.

Da SILVA
(rising) Where are they?

(The Doctor remains silent)

Where are they? I'm speaking to you!

DOCTOR
(frigidly) Constable—I am waiting for you to question me.

CONSTABLE
I can only repeat the gentleman's question—Where are they?

DOCTOR
At this point, my obligation to respond ceases until I know by what right you ask me this question.

Da SILVA
By what right? That young woman is my daughter—that masked man, her seducer.

DOCTOR
Your warrant.

CONSTABLE
Here it is, read it.

DOCTOR
"Order to arrest, wherever she may be found a young woman whose description follows"—her name is not here.

Da SILVA
Read.

DOCTOR
"The bearer of this warrant will himself designate the person against whom it must be executed." You are powerful, sir, to obtain such an order against a woman in a free country.

Da SILVA
Well, sir, my daughter—instantly!

DOCTOR
You shall see her, sir—I am unable to oppose it, but I cannot consent to your taking her away.

Da SILVA
And who will prevent me from it, since the King and the law wish it?

DOCTOR
I, sir, and on this occasion I am more powerful than the law and the King— I oppose it in virtue of my power as a doctor—and I declare it is impossible that this young woman follow anyone whoever he may be—even her father.

Da SILVA
Why's that?

DOCTOR
Because there would be danger of death for her to do it. to demand it would be an assassination, and in my turn, I will summon these gentlemen to lend me main force to protect a life for which, at the moment, I answer to God and men.

CONSTABLE
Explain yourself, Doctor.

DOCTOR
The young person you are pursuing just gave birth a few minutes ago.

Da SILVA
Curse on her if you are telling the truth! But you are lying to save her—and I forgive you everything for that.

ROBERTSON
(entering excitedly) Doctor! Doctor! Caroline and her child are in need of you.

(noticing Da Silva) God.

Da SILVA
(grabbing him by the collar) Stop!

ROBERTSON
(overwhelmed) The Marquis!

De SILVA
Wretch! I've got you now! My daughter?

DOCTOR
Gentlemen, gentlemen—such violence in my home!

Da SILVA
Leave us alone, Doctor. Infamous! Answer me!

ROBERTSON
Take care, sir! Respect and patience may escape me some day.

De SILVA
And then?

ROBERTSON
And then I will forget you are Caroline's father.

Da SILVA
And then?

ROBERTSON
Then you are still young enough, sir, for us to cross swords, or we can exchange bullets.

De SILVA
A duel! A duel with you! Oh, it's the mask hiding your face that gives you the boldness to speak that way to a man—Listen, I know who you are—Let's end this.

ROBERTSON
Damnation!

Da SILVA
My daughter!

CONSTABLE
(coming closer) Sir—we cannot suffer.

Da SILVA
Tell this man to keep off—that you do this of your own free will, Robert Fildy.

ROBERTSON
Fildy! No more doubt! Keep away, gentlemen, don't interfere, Doctor.

Da SILVA
Take me to my daughter.

ROBERTSON
The sight of you will kill her.

Da SILVA
Better a dead daughter than one dishonored, and dishonored by you.

ROBERTSON
Pity for her and kill me.

Da SILVA
She's there, isn't she?

ROBERTSON
Yes, but you cannot see her at his time.

Da SILVA
I will see her.

ROBERTSON
(before the door) Impossible.

Da SILVA
Who's going to prevent me from it?

ROBERTSON
Me!

Da SILVA
You defy me—?

ROBERTSON
I brave all for her!

Da SILVA
Stop—or I will tell who you are.

ROBERTSON
Stop—or I'll reveal—

Da SILVA
Well—?

ROBERTSON
Well—they will know that the daughter of the Marquis Da Silva d'Aguaroltes is the wife of—

Da SILVA
You shut up!

ROBERTSON
For she is my wife before God, and the child she has just born is your grandson.

Da SILVA
All the more reason that I see her.

ROBERTSON
You shall not see her.

Da SILVA
You'll have to murder me then.

ROBERTSON
If that's the only way.

Da SILVA
(in a loud voice) Caroline! Caroline!

CAROLINE
(off) My father!

ROBERTSON
Damnation! She heard that! Silence! Silence!

CAROLINE
(rushing from Mrs. Grey's room in disorder, falling at the feet of the Marquis) Father! Father!

MRS. GREY
(following her) What are you doing? Do you want to die?

CAROLINE
As heaven pleases!

ROBERTSON
All is lost.

DOCTOR
Don't worry, I won't leave her.

Da SILVA
Get up—

CAROLINE
Oh, no, no, I am fine here—at your feet, at your knees which I embrace.

Da SILVA
Unworthy child!

CAROLINE
Yes, yes, all on me, all on me, father! For he had only one fault—it was that I not reveal our love—

Da SILVA
She admits it.

CAROLINE
And why shouldn't I admit it, father? He is so brave and so generous.

Da SILVA
Him! Him! This one here!

CAROLINE
Yes, brave and generous! He saved my life, father. It happened when I fell from a boat in the Thames—He was passing by luckily—I told you I was saved by a stranger I hadn't seen again. I lied father, I saw him again—Father, he saved your daughter—Why think of it—

Da SILVA
Better to die than to owe your life to this man.

CAROLINE
I thought you loved me, father—When I saw him again, I wanted to tell you everything, he didn't wish it, why I don't know.

Da SILVA
Well, I know.

CAROLINE
I loved him as a savior, his elevated spirit, his noble face—all conspired to ruin me—Father! Father! Pardon us.

Da SILVA

Never!

CAROLINE
Robertson—oh, speak to him! Implore him on your behalf—the interest which attaches to a proscribed exile!

Da SILVA
Him, an exile?

CAROLINE
Yes, yes—that's why he's hiding himself—why this mask—

Da SILVA
He deceived you, child.

CAROLINE
But tell him, no, Robertson, tell him you didn't deceive me—! Oh—a word, a word!

Da SILVA
You see—he holds his peace.

CAROLINE
Robertson—a word—just one!

Da SILVA
Enough! Follow me.

CAROLINE
Father, I cannot—

Da SILVA
You really fear death!

CAROLINE
I'm afraid to leave him.

Da SILVA
Wretched girl! You love him so much?

CAROLINE
As I love the day, I love life, as I love God.

Da SILVA
But he's from hell— Come!

CAROLINE
And my child, my poor child!

DOCTOR
Unhappy mother.

Da SILVA
This Doctor will raise it.

DOCTOR
I receive this mission from heaven; he will be my son!

CAROLINE
(resisting) Oh, I cannot separate myself from my child—they can't separate a mother from her son—God gave him to her so she could nurse him with her milk. Oh! Let me at least bring my child!

Da SILVA
Impossible!

CAROLINE
I will call for help, father and everyone who has a heart will help me when I say, "Oh, look, look it's a mother weeping because they are taking her child from her that she's hardly seen, hardly embraced.

Da SILVA
(to the Constable) Gentlemen, help me.

(He wants to drag Caroline away)

MRS. GREY and THE DOCTOR
Pity! Pity for her!

ROBERTSON
(placing his hand on Da Silva's shoulder) Leave this young woman here.

CAROLINE
Oh—my father! My Robertson!

Da SILVA
Your Robertson—well, come everybody, let the whole world know about your Robertson—Take off the mask.

(tearing it off) Look—he's—

DOCTOR
(to the men who came forward) Oh, gentlemen, gentlemen—

ROBERTSON
Silence—in the name of your daughter and for your daughter—

(He replaces his mask, very quickly; there's only been time to glimpse his face.)

Da SILVA
You are right—she alone should know you.

(low to her)

CAROLINE
(anxiously) Well?

Da SILVA
He's the executioner.

CAROLINE
Ah.

(she falls in a faint)

CURTAIN

ACT I

Scene 1

Same set as the Prologue—only twenty years later.

Mawbray and Dr. Grey are playing chess. Mrs. Grey is working—Richard is writing.

MAWBRAY
No, Doctor, you are mistaken, my pawn was here, my knight there—I gave check with the Queen.

DOCTOR
And as for me, I took the Queen with the castle.

MAWBRAY
Indeed, no—

DOCTOR
Indeed, yes—

MAWBRAY
Let's put the pieces back where they were.

DOCTOR
Yes.

DOCTOR
That's fine. Richard, I make you the judge.

RICHARD
Oh, excuse me—father, I haven't followed your game—I'm doing some important and hurried work.

DOCTOR
Relative to elections?

RICHARD
Yes, father.

MRS. GREY
Cursed politics! Must I always hear talk of that?

JENNY
(entering) Father, your newspaper.

DOCTOR
Ah—give it to me.

JENNY
Good morning, Mama.

(kissing her on the face)

What are you doing there?

MRS. GREY
You see—cuffs for your father.

JENNY
They aren't as pretty as mine.

MAWBRAY
You're making some, too?

JENNY
Yes, for Richard, but you mustn't tell him, Mama, I want to surprise him.

DOCTOR
(reading) I'm with you, Mawbray.

JENNY
(going to Richard) Hello, Richard, hello.

RICHARD
Ah, it's sis—hello.

DOCTOR
By Saint George! Another one.

RICHARD
What's wrong, father?

DOCTOR
The opposition party has lost in Westmoreland!

RICHARD
What, the elections are already over! Who was nominated?

DOCTOR
 Lord Stapfort.

RICHARD
Imbeciles! A nobleman to represent the rights of the people! God damn me, I believe that if sheep could vote they'd nominate the butcher.

DOCTOR
It's our turn day after tomorrow.

RICHARD:
It won't be that way here, I hope. Lord for Lord, people for people, God for all, and the rights of each will be maintained.

MAWBRAY
The preparatory meeting of electors is going to take place. Do you think I could be present, Doctor?

DOCTOR: Why, not?

MAWBRAY
Stranger in this country, where only ten years ago I came to seek refuge after a long absence from England, I have no political rights.

DOCTOR
At this meeting all they do is argue, they don't vote.

MAWBRAY
Still, I tremble I'll be asked about my past life, about details of misfortunes, which are not personal to me, and I'm prevented from confiding them even to you.

DOCTOR: You'll do me the justice, Mawbray, that I've never asked you for an account of them. A simple life, gentle manners, your almost paternal affection for our children: that's what makes you our friend.

(Mawbray wants to reply. The Doctor, with friendship) Let's not discuss it any further.

(to Richard) Are you coming with us?

RICHARD
No question

DOCTOR
And to whom will you give your voice?

RICHARD
To myself, father, and I request yours and those of your friends.

MAWBRAY and DOCTOR
To you

JENNY
Richard, an M.P.?

RICHARD
Why no?

DOCTOR: And how long have you had that idea?

RICHARD
Since I started thinking about it.

DOCTOR
And your hopes date?

RICHARD
From yesterday.

DOCTOR
They rest?

RICHARD
On this letter.

MAWBRAY
An anonymous letter?

RICHARD
Anyway, read it.

DOCTOR (reading)
"You are young, passionate, ambitious; tomorrow the county names its representative: place yourself in the ranks. Mr. Grey and you exercise a great influence over the town-folk, and I have influence over the people, and we will carry your election by assault. I will see you tomorrow. You will learn the motives that cause me to act. I believe you are the man to understand them." And you trust this letter?

RICHARD
No one would have any interest in deceiving me. Many might desire that I succeed.

DOCTOR
Richard, you are very young.

RICHARD
Pitt was a minister at twenty-one.

MAWBRAY
But what guaranty will you offer the voters?

RICHARD
My past life.

DOCTOR
But you possess nothing.

RICHARD
You have some fortune.

MRS. GREY
But I thought the manufacturer Stillman was placing himself in the ranks.

RICHARD
The electors will fear he'll sell them out for a supply of wool.

DOCTOR
Wilkie, the Banker?

RICHARD
Well.

DOCTOR (taking Mawbray aside)
Isn't now the time to tell him he's not my son?

MAWBRAY
He will want to know who his father is, and you've told me you've nothing to tell him on that score.

JENNY (going to Richard)
Oh, Richard, if women voted!

DOCTOR
Yes, yes, that might rob him of his confidence, and I admit to you, Mawbray, I prefer to see him this way, confident in his strength, and conscious of his own merit.

MAWBRAY
My good doctor.

DOCTOR
Mawbray, we'll go listen to his maiden speech in Parliament. (to Richard) Well, Richard, so be it! I, too, had this dream, but I didn't think it would be accomplished so soon.

MRS. GREY
Mr. Mawbray, you won't leave my husband?

JENNY
Nor Richard?

MAWBRAY
Don't worry. I'll be present at this meeting as a disinterested spectator, since as a stranger to the county I have no political rights.

RICHARD
(looking at his watch) Come on, come on, let's go, it's time.

MRS. GREY
Goodbye then, gentlemen. But don't be late coming back.

JENNY
Good luck, Richard. Goodbye, goodbye!

(Richard, preoccupied, leaves with Mawbray and the Doctor without replying to Jenny)

JENNY
(eyes fixed on the door through which they've gone) Not a word! Not a look!

MRS.GREY
Well, Jenny?

JENNY
(shaking) Mother?

MRS. Grey
What are you doing there, motionless?

JENNY
I—I was thinking things over.

MRS. GREY
Indeed, I believe I've noticed for some time you've been really pensive; especially when Richard isn't here, you give yourself to reflections.

JENNY: Solitude is favorable to them.

MRS. GREY
Solitude! Well, what about me in that case?

JENNY: Oh, you are not some one—you—you are my mother.

MRS. GREY
Child, you ought not to let yourself go this way, to be too engrossed in your thoughts.

JENNY: Is it wrong to do?

MRS. GREY
That depends on their nature.

JENNY
Can't one think about her brother?

MRS. GREY
About her brother, yes, about Richard, no. Richard thinks he's your brother but you know he isn't. The secret was revealed to you as soon as you were capable of understanding the difference between affections owed to a brother and those owed to a friend.

JENNY
And why wasn't the secret revealed to Richard himself?

MRS. GREY
Mawbray always insisted to my husband that he be left in his ignorance.

JENNY
And that causes him to love me like a brother.

MRS. GREY
And how else would you want him to love you?

JENNY
Oh, pardon, mother, I am mad.

MRS. GREY
You see quite clearly that you are thinking aloud and that you are not alone.

JENNY
Mother, I've really wanted to cry—would that be wrong, too?

MRS. GREY
Ah, my child, keep your tears. God made them for real misfortune—and before the end of his life every man has occasion to pour his out.

JENNY
Mother—what can prevent happiness—?

MRS. GREY
It's that each of us dreams in his own way. Coordinating the series of events which must concur in it, thinking that fate will lend itself to his calculations in the future, then the future comes—and fate pushes down this house of cards. Your happiness—at least, the happiness you are dreaming of, is that of a peaceful life in the place where you were born, with your parents, having our little domain for your country, Richard, for your spouse—

JENNY
Well?

MRS. GREY
Well, my child, we are old, we are going to die.

JENNY
Well?

MRS. GREY
Richard will take you to London, and you will leave the country you were born in.

JENNY
Anywhere, anywhere with him!

MRS. GREY
His political pursuits will isolate you from each other—and more so each day. He cannot always stay near you, to give you the parents you have lost, the land you left, or the peace of mind that you won't know how to recover—

JENNY
Mama, my dream isn't yours— And haven't you been happy with father?

MRS. GREY
Mr. Gray wasn't ambitious, Jenny.

JENNY
Well, if what you tell me is true, mother, do you think the time for me to weep hasn't come yet?

MRS. GREY
Child, distract yourself, have you been occupied with this sketch for a long while?

JENNY
I haven't made much progress with it.

MRS. GREY
Your piano?

JENNY
I know all the sonatas Richard gave me—the others are too difficult.

MRS. GREY
You love him more than you ought to, my child.

JENNY
I'm afraid so, mother.

MRS. GREY
O' Jenny, what madness! Do you even know if he loves you?

JENNY
He thinks he's my brother, and he loves me like his sister.

MRS. GREY
And if after learning he is not your brother, he continues to love you like a brother?

JENNY
Mother—

MRS. GREY
Still, if that were so?

JENNY
Oh! I will be really wretched—

MRS. GREY
You see!

JENNY
Mother, pressed by your questions I am answering you without knowing what I'm saying to you—if I were alone a minute, if your presence didn't make me blush and trouble all my thoughts—I'd try to put myself in order—and when I see you again mother, I'll be more calm and probably more reasonable.

MRS. GREY
Well, my child, question your soul, don't rely on your strength more than you think you have the power to do—don't be more on guard against yourself than its reasonable to be—Think that a daughter has no better friend than her mother and that all is lulled in her arms—even remorse. Adieu, my child.

JENNY
Au revoir, mother.

(Mrs. Grey leaves.)

JENNY
Oh, Richard, Richard, if what my mother said is true, if you might never love me except as a brother, oh, I feel that that would be much too little to make me happy. Mother is right—does his hand tremble when it takes mine—while I am shaking throughout my body touching him? Does his heart beat, morning or night when he rests his lips on my face and I feel my heart inflate as if it were going to burst out of my breasts? No, he is calm, Richard, always calm, except when he's speaking of his plans for the future—that's when his soul lights up—that's when his eyes inflame. Just now the hope of being elected M.P. almost made him forget my existence—? Did he answer my goodbyes with words or looks? Oh, I have the strength to defend him against others—against myself, oh My God. I feel I don't— Oh—it's him—what's the matter with him?

RICHARD
(returning) Curses!

JENNY
How pale he is! How agitated he seems!

RICHARD
I could no longer bear it. To fail in this manner! And disgrace and derision! I am not the son of Dr. Grey!

JENNY
(letting out a cry) Ah!

RICHARD
It's you, Jenny! Did you know that I was not your brother?

JENNY
I knew it, Richard.

RICHARD
And you didn't tell me! And the doctor didn't tell me! And no friend told me— A stranger hurled this secret in my face like an insult, and each elector said, "It's true, he is not the son of Dr. Grey—He possesses neither name nor property—therefore, he cannot represent men who own property have a name." Do you know mine, Jenny?— You know it, tell me!

JENNY
Alas, no.

RICHARD
A second time, Jenny—tell me if you know—so I can go hurl myself in the midst of these insolent townsfolk and tell them, "I also, I have a name—and more than you, I have a soul which understands and a mind that thinks"— The imbeciles! "His family isn't known." The County is indeed happy to have given birth to the noble families of Stillman and Wilkie! Yes, I'm a stranger to the county and what does it matter if I lend to the county which has adopted me the strength of intelligence, and the power of talent! I don't possess anything—no, it's true, I have neither the factory of Mr. Stillman nor the bank of Mr. Wilkie— But I have a head which conceives and an arm which executes— It mustn't be thought of any more, never

think of it any more, Jenny! Do you understand this? To lose the hope of ten years in a minute—!!

JENNY
My friend.

RICHARD
Not to think of it anymore! When I feel in this face that burns my hand, the genius and the power to dominate that mob which judges and scorns me. Without that revelation to which your father didn't know how to respond, the masses were with me— The aristocratic pretensions of a tailor and the pride of a boot maker require that their representative reveal his breeding clearly unto the fourth generation! It's still this people with its need for despotism and its predilection for aristocracy; this people of Shakespeare who know no other way of rewarding Caesar's assassin than by making him Caesar! Oh! They are right to deceive you; they are avenging themselves on your blindness and escaping from you with ingratitude— And yet, with what power my voice would have thundered from the rostrum to defend your rights! My political notions would have soon embraced not only the interests of a puny village or a narrow county, but an entire nation. Oracle of a party, the others would have called me with their petitions, solicited by their promises— And I would have been master of old England, to choose at my fancy either to be the leader of the people—or on first steps of the throne. Curse on those cowardly townsfolk who clipped my wings without knowing they were those of an eagle.

A SERVANT
(entering) Mr. Richard.

RICHARD
(with asperity) What do you want with me?

SERVANT
There are several men who insist on speaking to you.

RICHARD
Who are they?

SERVANT
Some electors who are leaving the preparatory meeting.

RICHARD
Eh! What need have I of these condolences?

SERVANT
They say they have matters of the utmost importance to communicate to you.

RICHARD
Have them in then, may past resentments not compromise hopes for the future.

(Several townsfolk and Thompson enter.)

RICHARD
(going to them) Well, gentlemen, you see success eludes us; I say "us" because I found warm friends in you.

FIRST TOWNSMAN
Be sure of our regret—

RICHARD
I thank you. It's gratifying to excite the interest of those one esteems—the meeting of voters has dispersed, gentlemen?

SECOND TOWNSMAN
Yes, but without settling anything.

RICHARD
What! The choice is not made?

FIRST TOWNSMAN
We weren't able to hear ourselves— The choice of a candidate is an important thing—to oppose a ministry as corrupt as the one we have, and the powerful family of Derby which since there first was a House of Commons—has always filled it with its puppets.

RICHARD
What! You couldn't find anyone to run against their henchman, Sir Stansen whom they impose on us at every election.

SECOND TOWNSMAN
We have several running, but we aren't in agreement.

RICHARD
Mr. Wilkie offers himself.

SECOND TOWNSMAN
He's not an orator, and what we need is a man who talks and talks loud.

RICHARD
Mr. Stillman.

FIRST TOWNSMAN
All the cloth sellers have declared against him.

RICHARD
And why?

SECOND TOWNSMAN
They're afraid he'll sell his conscience for the title of army contractor.

RICHARD
Then, gentlemen, what procures me the pleasure of seeing you?

THOMPSON
(in a low voice) Get this young girl out of here.

RICHARD
Jenny, we're talking politics, this conversation has little interest for you, and perhaps, in front of you these gentlemen won't express themselves with complete freedom.

JENNY
I'll withdraw. Richard, be prudent.

RICHARD
Yes, yes.

(Jenny leaves.)

RICHARD
And as for me, gentlemen, do I owe my failure only to ignorance of my birth?

Richard Darlington, by Dumas & Dinaux * 49

SECOND TOWNSMAN
To that reason alone. You had all the opponents of Mr. Stillman and Wilkie for you—and that was the majority. The subscriptions underwriting the expenses of the election were increasing moment by moment—But many said "It'd impossible to elect a man who has no relatives attaching him to the county."

THOMPSON
(in a low voice) You could marry and have a family.

(Richard looks at Thompson)

FIRST TOWNSMAN
Still, they said, if only he owned property.

THOMPSON
(low again) If his father-in-law owned two or three factories.

RICHARD
(looks at Thompson penetratingly, then turns) And those are the only reasons that prevented my election?

FIRST TOWNSMAN
We don't know of any other.

RICHARD
If I removed these objections?

FIRST TOWNSMAN
Success would be certain.

RICHARD
And then I could count on you?

FIRST TOWNSMAN
And on our friends.

RICHARD
Well, gentlemen, tonight, I hope to have a change in my situation to announce to you. Will you meet me at the King's Arms at five o'clock?

THE TOWNSFOLK
That's agreed.

RICHARD
Accept my thanks, gentlemen.

(to Thompson) Stay, I have to talk to you. No goodbyes, gentlemen. At five o'clock.

(All but Thompson leave.)

RICHARD
You've been giving yourself a lot of trouble over my election, sir

THOMPSON
I had a hundred votes for you.

RICHARD
And can I know the nature of the interest, I inspire in you? For I don't have the honor of knowing you.

THOMPSON
It was I who wrote to you.

RICHARD
What motive made me worth the honor of your letter?

THOMPSON
Your character.

RICHARD
(smiling) Which is?

THOMPSON
Ambitious.

RICHARD
Who said I was?

THOMPSON
I've been watching you.

RICHARD
You are frank.

THOMPSON
I am blunt.

RICHARD
And you support your pretensions?

THOMPSON
With my head and my arm—like you.

RICHARD
And who are you?

THOMPSON
Nobody, like you.

RICHARD
And why do you think you need me to succeed?

THOMPSON
My position; some past events have taken away my hope of succeeding alone—I was born too near the people to be able to have directly exercised in me—the influence that I have on them. I have a hundred votes for you—I would have only one for myself.

RICHARD
Then you want to make a tool of me?

THOMPSON
No, a patron— You will be a warship and I will be the sloop that trails after; but pay attention, Sir Richard, in bad weather the sloop can save the crew.

RICHARD
And if I were to accept this treaty and we were to rise together—What would be my place?

THOMPSON
The first.

RICHARD
Always?

THOMPSON
Always—mine the second. Between the genius and the world which he moves, a lever is necessary.

RICHARD
You want to be the fairy's ring? Well, so be it—if I have the power.

THOMPSON
Your body and soul.

RICHARD
Our first means of succeeding?

THOMPSON
Your marriage with he doctor's daughter?

RICHARD
Nothing could be so simple—if the execution of the project didn't have to be in such haste.

THOMPSON
They love you too much not to hasten to agree.

RICHARD
The success couldn't be announced until it was too late for the election.

THOMPSON
True, if you had to wait to proclaim victory until it was earned.

RICHARD
In that case one needs a zealous friend mixing with the skeptical waters.

THOMPSON
Who would tell them the affair was concluded.

RICHARD
Who would speak of the doctor's wealth?

THOMPSON
Which is increasing by several pounds sterling in the bank.

RICHARD
And who will spread these rumors?

THOMPSON
I will. I take on those functions today.

RICHARD
Our agreements in advance.

THOMPSON
To Richard, private person—Thompson, valet; to Richard, Proprietor, Thompson, his manager; to the Honorable Sir Richard, M.P., Thompson, his Secretary; to Lord Richard, Minister, Thompson, whatever Milord wishes— Arrived at the conclusion—to divvy up the reward—Richard is too clever not to be grateful.

RICHARD
So be it. Shake!

THOMPSON
Goodbye for now.

RICHARD
You're leaving?

THOMPSON
You need me to be at the Arms of the King pub.

(he leaves.)

RICHARD
Intriguing lieutenant! One who doesn't want any money! Forever the valet, never a rival! That's the man I need—Jenny!

JENNY
They brought you good news?

RICHARD
Why, dear Jenny?

JENNY
I left you sad and find you happy again.

RICHARD
My joy comes from myself, Jenny, and not from others.

JENNY
I don't understand.

RICHARD
Jenny, I am not the son of the doctor.

JENNY
And that makes you happy? Bad son! Bad brother!

RICHARD
Oh, yes indeed, bad brother, Jenny.

JENNY
What's caused this sudden change in your soul?

RICHARD
This secret.

JENNY
You knew it when you returned—and your face was confused.

RICHARD
You're not speaking to me in the intimate way you used to, Jenny.

JENNY
You're no longer my brother, Richard.

RICHARD
Your hand, Jenny!

JENNY
My hand?

RICHARD
(aside) She's trembling.

(aloud) I know the happiest of men.

JENNY
What a change!

RICHARD
Oh, bad luck to me if you don't understand.

JENNY
(pulling her hand away) Sir—

RICHARD
When I came back that secret was resounding in my brain. I was struck by lightening—I wasn't yet able to get my thoughts together. I fled like a ruined man, for at first sight this secret stole everything from me—A social position, adored parents, a cherished sister—a sister—I hung up on this word— And I looked clearly into my soul. How many times, without fathoming the reason—had this word "sister" made me sad when I uttered it. How many times looking at you had I become thoughtful! I would say to myself, "She's my sister"— And I'd withdraw from you with fear in my heart that was almost remorse— This vague torment, that I dared not investigate, made me fanciful. My soul burned, and I attempted to appear cold—or preoccupied— For if you had been truly my sister, Jenny, and you were experiencing what I was experiencing, that in taking my hand I felt it tremble as it is doing now—

JENNY
Richard.

RICHARD
If I'd felt your heart jump—as it is doing now—

JENNY
Leave me alone.

RICHARD
When I was coming close to give you a kiss from a brother.

(he takes her in his arms)

JENNY
My God! My God!

RICHARD
If instead of meeting your cheek, I had touched your lips.

(They kiss.)

JENNY
(pulling away) Ah!

RICHARD
Well, now, Jenny—instead of crime—there's joy—Instead of guilt, there's happiness because love I you Jenny—I love you like a madman—And if you were my sister, death alone could save me from a crime.

JENNY
Oh, mercy! Mercy! Pity.

RICHARD
Oh, yes—pity for me, Jenny—For I who am dying and waiting for a word from you to live—Oh, answer, answer—

JENNY
Can I do it? Oh, this is a delirium. I've lost my head. I am crazy!

RICHARD
Jenny, Jenny—do you love me?

JENNY
Do I love him! He asks that!

RICHARD
Oh, my Jenny! My love!

JENNY
(noticing the doctor and Mawbray entering) Father!

(she runs off)

RICHARD
(aside) This will save me an explanation lasting a quarter of an hour.

DOCTOR
Well, Richard, what's the meaning of this?

(to Mawbray) He didn't waste any time.

RICHARD
Father, my friend, I'm not trying to deny it or defend myself.

DOCTOR
That, it seems to me, would be difficult.

RICHARD
Anyway, I am too happy to be able to repent!

DOCTOR
As for me, Richard, as father, I have the right to complain.

RICHARD
Oh, from the moment this secret was revealed to me—that I was not your son, I was no longer able to resist a frightful idea—that Jenny would always see a brother in me—even though she had ceased to be my sister.

DOCTOR
And that was what made you leave the meeting like a madman—to abandon the game which was only half lost?

RICHARD
Eh, father, party, election, the realm—what does all that matter? All that had vanished before a single idea: that of returning to be what I'd always thought I was—your son—separate you from the name of "father"? Couldn't I say "father" for father-in-law?

DOCTOR
Eh! What the devil! Say it forever—I am as accustomed to it as you—And it would cost me more perhaps, "My Son!" But for this to be two things are necessary: Jenny's love—

RICHARD
Oh, she loves me—father, she loves me— She told me so.

DOCTOR
And her mother's consent— Her mother whose rights you are forgetting, Richard.

RICHARD
Father, I'd forgotten the whole world so as to remember only Jenny.

DOCTOR
Richard, tell my wife I'm waiting for her.

RICHARD
I will tell her—f—

DOCTOR
Well—

RICHARD
F—

DOCTOR
Father—come on—

RICHARD
(throwing himself in his arms) Father.

(he leaves.)

MAWBRAY
Well, my friend?

DOCTOR
He deserved that lesson.

MAWBRAY
Which one?

DOCTOR
The one I just gave him.

MAWBRAY
And you call that a lesson?

DOCTOR
Eh! Why should I have been more severe when that rascal has taken it into his head to realize in one shot all the hopes of fifteen years, my plans for the future, a dream that I only abandoned when I

thought Richard paid little attention to my daughter? True God, Mawbray. I am delighted to be mistaken.

(Mrs. Grey enters)

MRS. GREY
You asked for me, my friend?

DOCTOR
Yes, my dear Anna, I have need of your help. Now's the moment to realize one of our most cherished dreams.

MRS. GREY
Which is?

DOCTOR
Jenny is seventeen; Richard is twenty-six.

MRS. GREY
Well—

DOCTOR
My dear Anna, it's the same age we were when we got engaged. What would you say to an anniversary?

MRS. GREY
Richard—Jenny's spouse?

DOCTOR
What is there to astonish you in that? Didn't you tell me twenty times yourself that this plan would be the happiness of our old age if it succeeded.

MRS. GREY
In the past—But haven't you noticed for a long time, my friend, that I no longer mention it to you?

DOCTOR
And why?

MRS. GREY
My friend—Richard's character has developed over the years—I followed his character with the soul and the eye of a mother.

DOCTOR
Well—

MRS. GREY
Well, my friend, he is ambitious.

DOCTOR
And you fear that passion?

MRS. GREY
For Jenny.

DOCTOR
It's the source of greatness, virtues.

MRS. GREY
And sometimes, great crimes—If this marriage were ever to cause unhappiness to our daughter—

DOCTOR
This unhappiness is even more certain if they are separated—Anna, our children love each other—

MRS. GREY
And how do you know it? Two hours ago Richard still thought he was our son.

DOCTOR
Well, ten minutes ago, I surprised our son at the feet of our daughter. Are we going to cause misfortune for these children?

MRS. GREY
If I were sure Jenny would be happy.

DOCTOR
She will be— We'll profit by the noble spirit in Richard's heart to inspire him to noble deeds—And if that keeps him off the path to wealth, we will always be there to help him.

MRS. GREY
And if God calls us to him?

DOCTOR
Our friend, Mawbray, will be there to replace us and watch over our child if she is in need.

MAWBRAY
I take a formal oath to do it before heaven.

MRS. GREY
Come, I really want that. Heaven has even blessed what you have done.

DOCTOR
(hugging his wife) It is you who deserve its blessing.

(Richard enters.)

DOCTOR
Ah! You're eavesdropping are you?

RICHARD
Forgive me, father, the time seemed so long to me.

MRS. GREY
Well, my friend, we consent.

RICHARD
I know mother, but I don't wish to spare myself the joy of hearing it form your own mouth. Do you want me to owe everything in my life to you, father?

DOCTOR
Didn't you foresee my response?

RICHARD
I feared that some obstacle that I didn't know, stemming from my family or from my birth. Do you allow me to go tell this news to Jenny?

DOCTOR
Not yet, my friend. You just spoke of your family and your birth. That's a subject I've always avoided discussing with you—I found it simpler—and especially so, when my heart called you my son. For what could I reveal to you since all was doubt and uncertainty? Be-

sides, I was hoping still that some event would come to put off the day of this adventure. Since heaven has not willed it so—the moment has come to tell you—everything—I am going to tell you, at least, what I remember—

(to Mawbray who grows pale and wishes to withdraw) Stay, Mawbray, I have nothing to say that Richard or I need blush about.

RICHARD
Father, I am listening to you.

DOCTOR
Twenty-six years ago, toward ten in the evening, a carriage stopped in front of this house. A masked man presented himself.

(Mawbray perks up)

Imploring my assistance for a young woman who accompanied him and who appeared to be in the final stages of her pregnancy. At the behest of this man, and without his unmasking, the young woman whose face was as pretty as her voice was sweet, was installed in the room today occupied by Mrs. Grey—

(Mawbray is noticeably moved)

Providence exacted our prayers—I received in my arms a child whose mother covered it with kisses and tears—That child, Richard was you!

RICHARD
Did the carriage which brought my mother display any arms—?

DOCTOR
(reflecting) Indeed that would have been a way of recognition, but no, I remember it didn't.

RICHARD
Another hope dashed! Continue, father, I beseech you.

DOCTOR
Hardly had your mother given you birth, poor child when someone knocked a second time at the door: these were the police who obeyed a man accompanied by a constable— He showed me a court

order to place the young girl who was in my house in his hands. I refused; he claimed her as a father— And at his voice, your mother, weak and trembling fell at his feet— The stranger gave the order that she be carried to his carriage.

MAWBRAY
(aside) Poor Caroline!

RICHARD
And my father—what did he do?

DOCTOR
He wanted to defend her, he approached the stranger with this end for he seemed to love your mother passionately.

MAWBRAY
(overwhelmed, aside) Oh, yes, passionately.

DOCTOR
The stranger was stopped by a word we couldn't hear— He tottered and fell annihilated into this chair.

(As they turn, they notice Mawbray unable to resist his emotion, has fallen into the chair that the doctor indicated)

MRS. GREY
What's the matter, Mawbray?

DOCTOR
He's ill.

MRS. GREY
(calling) Jenny, Jenny, my smelling salts!

DOCTOR
Mawbray, Mawbray, my friend!

JENNY
What's wrong, mother?—Oh, my God! I'm all atremble.

DOCTOR
Our friend has just fainted, but it will be nothing.

MAWBRAY
No, my friend, no—a passing flash—

JENNY
Oh, Mama, when I heard you call this way I was very frightened—
It's really quite wrong, Mr. Mawbray to frighten your friend so.

MRS. GREY
I am all ashamed of the trouble I am causing you. I interrupted you—continue, my friend, I am better—completely better—

DOCTOR
I didn't have anything more of interest to say.

RICHARD
Never mind, father, continue.

DOCTOR
I'll finish then—after the scene I just spoke of—I never again saw your father or your mother— Only at regular intervals I received sums of money through the post sufficient for your upkeep. Around ten years ago, shortly before the arrival of Mawbray in this town, I received 5,000 pounds sterling with the announcement that this would be the last that I could receive. Since that time, all my inquires have been useless— And so I thought our adoption of you was forever ratified by your parents.

MAWBRAY
(shaking the doctor's hand) Noble and generous friend!

RICHARD
Well, are you still astonished, father that I want to be connected to you by another bond?

DOCTOR
No, but Jenny might refuse.

JENNY
(in her mother's arms) Oh, Mama, I didn't say that.

DOCTOR
So, if I say to Richard, "Be my daughter's spouse" you won't make me a liar?

JENNY
Have I ever disobeyed you, father?

DOCTOR
Well, all that was lacking was your consent.

RICHARD
You hear, Jenny, your consent.

JENNY
Richard, my friend, you know quite well I no longer need to give it.

DOCTOR
(in a gentle but solemn voice) Richard, in the presence of our best friend, the only witness of this sacred engagement, my wife and myself give you what we hold dearest in the world—our child. Take the rights of a spouse over her—We abandon to you those rights that we have by nature; her happiness has been our thought at all times, in our prayers every evening—You replace us now, my friend, look at those tears in the eyes of your adoptive mother, listen to my trembling voice! Oh, I beg you, Richard, make Jenny happy and you will make us so!

MAWBRAY
(seizing Richard's arm) Richard, this prayer from a father is heard in heaven!

RICHARD
(pointing to his heart) And here, sir.

MRS. GREY
Jenny, be a good wife.

JENNY
I will imitate you, mother.

RICHARD
Oh, Jenny! All the days of my life are yours! Let all my ambitious plans die—! Do I need anything when you belong to me?

DOCTOR
That's the way with young folks—extreme in everything. Well, no, sir, you shan't renounce your plans when their success is more than

probable. Your success is no longer yours alone—half belongs to Jenny—she has the right to claim it.

RICHARD
You want it, father! But to separate myself from her so soon! Jenny.

JENNY
My Richard.

DOCTOR
Come on—go before—we'll rejoin you.

RICHARD
You want it then, Jenny?

(aside) Five o'clock—just in time.

(aloud) Goodbye then! Stansen. has his colors, I need mine.

(taking Jenny's belt) Here they are!

ALL
Good luck!

RICHARD
Oh—everything has to succeed for me, this is my lucky day!

(He leaves by the street door. The family withdraws by a side door.)

BLACKOUT

ACT I

Scene 2

The public square in Darlington. In the background, the King's Arms pub. In the forefront, a hall with a balcony— To the audience's left, the Marlborough pub also with a projecting balcony— On the right the hustings and benches leaning against the house— In front of the benches tables protected by barriers—a trellis four feet high— Most of the windows are hung with flags, some blue, others yellow.

Thompson, Richard, Voters, townsfolk, a female merchant of blue ribbons, and a female merchant of yellow ribbons—There is a crowd sporting the different colors in their hats, buttonholes, each representing their candidates. In the room at the Kings Arms, Thompson is seated at a table, surrounded by townsfolk, partisans of Richard— some write, others fold papers. Thompson unfolds a box of placards to a poster man, who sorts them and distributes them around the square—Richard's name can be seen in large letters—A poster-man at the Marlborough leaves with posters on which Stansen's name can be seen. Curiosity seekers group themselves around the posters.

FARMER
(to a voter with blue colors who is part of a group) Can you point me, sir, to Mr. Richard's committee?

VOTER
It's here at the Arms of the King—do you have any news?

FARMER
None—just get here—I'm coming to donate fifty pounds sterling to the expenses off the election.

VOTER
(to the others wearing his colors) Bravo, my friends! He's one of ours! And don't you have a blue ribbon? I want to give you one, I do.

(goes to the ribbon girl) Hey! Mistress—two cuts of blue ribbon.

RIBBON GIRL
Go elsewhere, radical! I only sell yellow ribbons.

ANOTHER RIBBON GIRL
As for me, I'm giving them away for nothing, to those who will support the election of Mr. Richard.

THE BLUE VOTERS
Long live the Ribbon girl.

(They've put ribbons on the hat and button of the farmer and escort him into the King's Arms. Several groups of Blues appear at the entrance to an abutting side street shouting, "There's Mr. Richard! There's Mr. Richard!")

(Richard enters, accompanied by three supporters carrying his colors—one of them holds a register—Thompson comes out on the balcony on hearing the commotion in the square.)

THOMPSON
Well, Mr. Richard, your visits?

RICHARD
The majority is mine.

BLUE VOTERS
Yahoo!

THOMPSON
And Mr. Stansen?

RICHARD
I just noticed him, finishing his turn in your street— As for me, I no longer have to see the electors who live there.

THOMPSON
Our committee hasn't wasted its time, everything is ready and we've just answered the last pamphlet of Mr. Stansen.

RICHARD
Very fine.

THOMPSON
Go—finish your visits—and good luck!

RICHARD
In a quarter of an hour, I will rejoin you.

(Thompson goes back into his room. Richard, with his committeemen goes toward the shop at the left, bearing the sign Blankfort, Shoemaker. A committeeman raps on the door.)

BLANKFORT
(opening) What can I do for you, sir?

COMMITTEEMAN
Mr. Blankfort?

BLANKFORT
That's me, sir.

RICHARD
(coming forward) Mr. Blankfort, I present myself to you as the candidate of commerce and industry.

(Mrs. and Miss Blankfort come to the door of the shop to listen to what is said.)

BLANKFORT
(who has listened attentively) You've got it.

RICHARD
(To the committeeman with the register) Inscribe Mr. Blankfort.

(to Blankfort) I thank you.

(offering his hand) Mrs. Blankfort allows me—

(embraces her) Miss is already too good an Englishman not to allow it—

(Richard embraces Miss Blankfort, too—and shakes Blankfort's hand again as he leaves. Blankfort goes back into his shop with his family. The Committeeman knocks on the door of the Marlborough Pub)

COMMITTEEMAN
Mr. Outram?

OUTRAM
(coming out) Here I am, sir.

RICHARD
Mr. Outram, called by a great member of my fellow citizens to the honor of the candidacy, I attach great importance to the role of a friend of Old England not to hurry to come ask you for yours.

OUTRAM
Mr. Richard, I will see you with pleasure elected by Darlington, but I have engagements. My tavern is hosting the Committee of Mr. Stansen.

RICHARD
Mr. Outram, I thank you.

(The Committeeman goes to rap at the neighboring house, and this repeats itself until the arrival of the High Bailiff. As Mr. Outram goes back as voters for Stansen call him.)

VOTER
Mr. Outram!

OUTRAM
What's the matter?

VOTER
Do you know if the committee still has enough to eat and drink?

OUTRAM
I've distributed to some questionable characters all the lunch and dinner—but I still have some pots of ale—Are you alone?

VOTER
Yes.

OUTRAM
I've need food for four people.

VOTER
I'm going to eat it all.

(All the voters wearing yellow ribbons come to one of the streets which abuts on the square, shouting, "Mr. Stansen! Here's Mr. Stansen"—Stansen enters with his committeemen one of whom has a register.)

OUTRAM
Be welcome, Sir Stansen. And your visits?

STANSEN
The majority is with me.

(shouts) Are the gentlemen of the committee still there?

OUTRAM
They spent the whole night delivering brochures and posters.

STANSEN
I'm going to thank them.

(to the voters who surround him) Till later, my friends. The High Bailiff is coming and the decisive moment is not far off.

(Stansen with his committeemen go into the Marlborough Pub. Bands announce the arrival of electors—yellows and blues with banners bearing inscriptions: Richard and Reform—Richard forever—Stansen and Derby—Stansen and the constitution. Some have posters with the names of their candidates wrapped onto their hats—others carry similar placards atop long poles. The High Bailiff enters with his old fashioned magistrate's costume. The listings are filled with spectators, among whom are seen the Doctor, Mawbray, Anna and Jenny Grey, the windows of the houses are filled with women and children. The shops are locked up.)

(Richard and Stansen appear on the balconies of their respective taverns.)

RICHARD
(noticing the Doctor and his family) My friends, I'm with you.

DOCTOR, MAWBRAY, JENNY
Hello, Hello—

(they wave their kerchiefs)

STANSEN
(from his balcony) My friends, relief is coming to you from the extremity of the country. I had them brought by boat, whose captain is devoted to me. He is bringing reinforcements of sixty votes.

RICHARD
Father—my good mother! Jenny!

DOCTOR
Well!

RICHARD
Everything is going well—Jenny, you will be the wife of an M.P.

JENNY
So long as my husband is called Richard Darlington, that's all that I desire.

RICHARD
And you, father—what have you done for me?

DOCTOR
I spent some time with my solicitor and—

RICHARD
But about the election?

DOCTOR
I've seen your friends—they've promised me ten votes.

JENNY
(joyously to Richard) Richard, the contract is already prepared.)

RICHARD
(distractedly) Very nice.

(to doctor) Father, you'll announce my marriage publicly won't you if you see it may become necessary for my election?

DOCTOR
Don't worry—

RICHARD
(going to Jenny and presenting her to the voters) Greet these gentlemen, Jenny—I just announced to them that tomorrow you will be my wife.

(Jenny curtsies—Richard receives congratulations from his friends)

THOMPSON
Master!

RICHARD
What's the matter?

(A barge is arriving full of Yellows, shouting, "Long live Stansen!")

THOMPSON
Bad luck! What to do? Take two hundred pounds sterling, get in a boat, reach the other barge—two hundred pounds sterling to the captain to deposit them on the opposite shore or in the sea, let them land anywhere but here.

THOMPSON
I'm running.

(He disappears.)

RICHARD
Forgive me, my friends, if I leave you, but you see something has to be done on every side.

ALL
Goodbye, goodbye—good luck.

(Richard and Stansen, with their friends, appear on their respective balconies.)

HIGH BAILIFF
(after having demanded silence) People of Darlington, two candidates present themselves to be elected to the House of Commons—Mr. Richard and Mr. Stansen—let them be heard in silence.

(The High Bailiff sits down—Richard indicates by his gestures that he wishes to speak. The band stops—the entire crowd turns to his side.)

RICHARD
Noble citizens of Old England.

(yahoos, hurrahs, huzzahs, voices calling for silence)

This is a strange spectacle for you—for a new man to dispute the seat of Mr. Stansen—who's held his seat in the House of Commons for thirty-five years, yes, for all that time, the Derby's wandering about our country could say, "These forests, rivers, towns and valleys belong to us"—they could also say and they do say, "The representatives of this country must belong to us."

DIVERSE VOICES
No! No! Yes! Yes!

RICHARD
You deny it in vain! The county has seven seats in Parliament, the Derbys sent their seven damned, souls, henchmen to it, it's hell represented by seven deadly sins—

(huzzahs, whistles, applause)

Their reign is over—a simple lawyer—me—your man—your creation—I dare to contend with them—because you have understood your rights, because you've said to yourself, "Everything belongs to us, we are richer than they are—since liberty is bought with guineas, we'll give some money."

(bravos—almost universal)

With our modest subscriptions, we will laugh at the 100,000 pounds sterling of the Derbys—you want gold go to the Derbys—that's their color! Blue citizens—you want your rights—put on mine; raise for me your arms and hands with votes—and I will give you my life to defend them.

(whistles, hurrahs)

Sir Stansen, you already picture yourself seated at your ease in the chair where the newly elected are carried triumphantly—but before you fall back into your spectral sleep, I'm coming to help you a bit—Cast aside your modesty; tell us what you have done for us—celebrate your battles—show us your body wearied by toil.

(general laughter)

Come, let Darlington be happier than Westminster. Let it hear your voice, and to purchase that privilege of going to the House after seven years of being silent— Shout lustily for once in broad daylight!

(laughter, stirrings of discontent from the Yellows)

Fellow citizens, Mr. Stansen has the past on his side, I have only the future—Despite this difference try to have an M.P. who body and soul is yours—who will defend inch by inch your rights, your money, that after each session will come tell you—"Here's what I have done—are you happy?"

(As soon as he finishes speaking, all the electors turn towards Stansen's balcony.)

STANSEN
People of Darlington, to condemn the audacity of the attempt made today.

(whistles, applause, Stansen repeats the phrase)

I don't wish to accuse my opponent for what has taken place in this square today.

CONFUSED VOICES
What's so terrible about that? Whyzzat? Shut up! Silence!

STANSEN
Compare this tumult, these preparations for war to the calm of our last elections.

(laughter, noise)

SEVERAL VOICES
Silence! They let Mr. Richard speak.

STANSEN
Well, you permit the first audacious passer-by to the trouble the peace of our county?

(shouts, huzzahs)

THOMPSON
(going to Richard) Englishman—silence! Noise gives Mr. Stansen a headache.

(laughter)

STANSEN
Since when has one dared to speak with such irreverence of the noble family of Derby—the most beautiful, the most ancient diamond in the crown of England?

VOICES
Bravo! Bravo!

OTHER VOICES
What's that to us?

STANSEN
For three hundred years, the Derbys have been our masters.

(An explosion by the Blues with Thompson at their head. "No more Masters! We don't want any masters!" Huzzahs, whistles! Stansen, despite being urged by his friends, gestures that he relinquishes the floor—but during the tumult, the Blues have rushed toward the placards bearing Stansen's name, tearing them down, stamping them underfoot—the debris is hurled against the unfortunate orator.)

HIGH BAILIFF
(reestablishing silence) You've heard the candidates—let those who are of the opinion to nominate Mr. Richard raise their hands.

(a large number of hands are raised)

Those who are of the opinion to nominate Mr. Stansen raise their hands.

(huzzahs, shouts—a lesser number of hands)

My opinion is that Mr. Richard has been named member for the village of Darlington.

(prolonged applause)

ONE OF STANSEN'S COMMITTEEMEN
(from the balcony) We demand the calling, the poll.

HIGH BAILIFF
Mr. Stansen demands the calling—the candidates have named their poll offices.

RICHARD, STANSEN, and their FRIENDS
Yes, yes, we are ready—

SEVERAL PERSONS
(near the tables) We are here.

HIGH BAILIFF
Gentlemen, you can open the poll. If a quarter of an hour passes without a voter presenting himself to be counted, the poll will close—Those who wish to check the rights of the voters come to the gates—

(General uproar—Richard, Stansen, and their friends descend to the square—their balconies are soon filled with the curious. Thompson can be seen in the midst of partisans of both candidates turning towards the polling tables and establishing himself on one of the benches overlooking them.

Other electors crowd around the barriers to watch the vote. Meanwhile, the whole crowd is in motion, they tear up banners in a struggle that is almost everywhere coming to an exchange of fists. When calm is somewhat restored, one can see, after much effort, four voters penetrate the barriers—among them is Dr. Grey.

Each swears, kissing the bible that he has not let himself be corrupted, they give their names. their residence and the vote—which are inscribed by the officials. Other voters replace them—Those mounted on the balustrades count the votes, and from time to time, in a loud voice, make known the result—)

THOMPSON
(to a voter who presents himself) You're not a freeholder; you're a servant of Lord Derby.

SERVANT
That's true, but I'm a proprietor with an income of forty shillings.

THOMPSON
Where's your shop?

SERVANT
About ten leagues from here, on the road to London, I think.

THOMPSON
What do you mean, you think? You've never been there?

SERVANT
No, I rent it.

THOMPSON
To whom do you rent it?

SERVANT
I don't know.

THOMPSON
Well, who pays you your rent?

SERVANT
Lord Derby's intendant.

THOMPSON
Gentlemen—I call your attention to the fraud.

YELLOW VOTERS
He's in order! He must vote.

THOMPSON and RICHARD'S PATRONS
This is base! This is terrible!

(A carriage full of porters brings in Blue voters who are greeted with applause by their own and with hoots by the Yellows. Meanwhile the polling continues. Thompson, with his friends, exhort those who appear to hesitate and applaud those who vote for Richard. The partisans of Stansen meddle around their side. A second carriage covered with posters brings reinforcements for Stansen—whose partisans receive them with hurrahs—in the midst of hoots from their adversaries.)

THOMPSON
(rushing from the benches and jumping in a cask) This count continues, Mr. Bailiff.

(general activity of curiosity)

SEVERAL VOICES
What's wrong?

(the High Bailiff appears.)

THOMPSON
Mr. Bailiff, in the expectation that everything would take place in good faith and honesty, I didn't wish to draw any distinctions between Protestants and Catholics, but we know that promises were made by Mr. Stansen, to the Papists—here's the servant presenting himself to vote. We insist that the oath of loyalty be exacted.

NUMEROUS VOICES
It's too late. He had to insist on the oath before the polling! You no longer have the right.

OTHER VOICES
No Papists! Down with the Papists, Stansen! Long live our Protestant religion.

(meanwhile, Thompson has had a lively exchange with the Bailiff who demands silence)

HIGH BAILIFF
The law being silent as to what moment the oath of supremacy must be demanded, we grant Sir Richard's demand. In consequence, each voter, before voting, shall declare on oath that he doesn't recognize the Pope as having any power spiritual or temporal, and that the doctrine of transubstantiation is damnable.

(This declaration is followed by a violent tumult and shouts on all sides. Thompson looks for Richard in the midst of the crowd and comes forward.)

THOMPSON
(with excitement) Prolong the disorder—there goes the election.

(Richard disappears for a few moments in the midst of the groups and then can be heard.)

RICHARD
I want to speak! I want to speak!

(Several of his friends point him toward the carriage and with their aid he gets on top of it and from there harangues the crowd)

My brave friends—if it was only a question of my interests I would have said already, "Give way to the injustice and the violence." But for your sake, I am ready to suffer everything—it's no longer a question of paying the most outrageous of budgets—have you ever calculated this budget? Do you know that in copper money it would go round the earth twenty-eight times?

SEVERAL VOICES
Ah! Good God! That's horrible! Is it possible?

RICHARD
But let's only speak of our country. If what we pay were counted in a straight line on a great highway—do you know how many times it would take to run through it?

VOICES
No, no—look, tell us!

RICHARD
You are good hikers in Northumberland?

VOICES
Yes, yes.

RICHARD
But, starting every morning you wouldn't do more than thirty-six miles a day.

VOICES
No! That's so! He's right!

RICHARD
Well—the voyage of our budget would take a rural postman 692 days—a year, ten months, twenty-seven days.

VOICES
It's inconceivable! What a calculation, he's a real brain!

RICHARD
What do I want, I who pay as you do?

VOICES
Ah, yes, you pay a lot.

RICHARD
To shorten some miles from the length of this interminable ribbon.

(pulling a stone from his pocket)

Here's how they thank me. A stone thrown against me, me who you applauded, me who your hands have proclaimed your representative. To defeat their adversary, they will murder him.

(This accusation by Richard excites the tumult to even more violence than all that preceded it, shouts, threats, are exchanged between the parties. Mr. Stansen is apostrophized in the most lively manner. "Coward, Brigand! Rogue!" His partisans protect him!)

STANSEN
(to his followers) Bring a table.

(Defended by them, he mounts a table where they were voting—and reestablishes silence after considerable trouble.)

THOMPSON
(looking at his watch) Ten minutes.

(He goes to the High Bailiff and shows him the watch.)

STANSEN
(vehemently) This is too much! Rage will give me the voice they say I lack. Englishmen don't reproach yourself for the rest of your lives for being tricked by a wretch who renders you his dupes— Your well being, your peace matters little to him—! But to him, honors, riches. He will defend your fortunes—him? That bastard! Does he know what a fortune is? Has he any patrimony? Has he got a family? No, he lies even when he says he is the son of the doctor, I—

(Explosion: "Yes! Yes! No! No!" Richard, Thompson, the Doctor want to speak—but noise prevents them—finally the Doctor speaks in a deep voice.)

DOCTOR
No—he's not my son.

VOICES
Ah! Ha!

DOCTOR
But he is my son-in-law.

OTHER VOICES
Ah! Ah! Bravo!

STANSEN
In adopting him, has Mr. Grey given him his virtues? Several of you know him already—of the deadly sins, they say he has only one— but the father has all the others—pride. Through pride he shouts at you! Through pride he will betray you—through pride—through pride.

(Thompson approaches the Bailiff anew and points to his watch. The polling is stopped.)

HIGH BAILIFF
(interrupting Stansen) The polls are closed.

STANSEN
Wait a minute! I am waiting for forty voters who are coming from the upcountry—in a sloop I chartered.

THOMPSON
Sir Stansen, if your brig has a good wind, your voters are by now well out to sea.

A YELLOW ELECTOR (running)
Sir Stansen, the sloop passed without disembarking—despite the shouts of the passengers—he added sail and soon we won't be able to see him.

STANSEN
Why he's a cheat—a cut-throat, this is a betrayal!

HIGH BAILIFF
For more than a quarter of an hour, no elector has presented himself to give his vote. I am gong to know the result of the poll.

(Deep silence. The poll officers bring the Bailiff their registers.)

HIGH BAILIFF
The result of the poll is—for Mr. Richard, 142 voices—for Mr. Stansen, 137. In consequence, Mr. Richard is proclaimed Representative of the town of Darlington

(Explosion of applause and boos, but soon the Yellows are chased off by the Blues. Mr. Stansen retires to the Marlborough Pub. Richard thanks his friends and gives his hand to those who surround him and goes to embrace his adoptive family.)

NUMEROUS VOICES
The triumph chair—the triumph chair.

(They bring a large armchair on a sort of shield and invite Richard to set on it.)

THOMPSON

(giving him his hand) Sir Member of Parliament.

RICHARD
Thanks, my Secretary.

THOMPSON
Take your seat in the House of Commons.

RICHARD
(getting up) It's the stair to the Lords—

(While they carry Richard around the square, music plays on all sides—they waive banners on the square, from windows and throw hats decorated with ribbons in the air—the ladies wave their kerchiefs—and in the midst of the hurrahs, Richard gives thanks to the crowd which cheers him.

CURTAIN

ACT II

Scene 3

A rostrum in the House of Commons reserved for Ministers and Lords, the door at the back allows one to see the house. The President is seated—he alone is visible—a murmur reveals that the back benches are filled although the members cannot be seen. At the beginning of the act, a curtain prevents the audience from seeing the commons. Mawbray, leaning against the wall, looks through the half opened curtain—one can hear the deep voice of Richard.

USHER
(looking at Mawbray) Good! He's following my recommendation and has not drawn the curtain. With his traveling clothes, I wouldn't care for him to be seen in the cabinet of the Ministers—but he can no longer remain here. Sir Richard is coming to the end of his speech which will soon terminate—he'll want to go into the chamber so I must warn him—Sir—

MAWBRAY
(almost without being disturbed) I am with you.

USHER
He seems to take a great interest in the bill under discussion—he's some government contractor.

(Cheers and applause can be heard in the House.)

USHER
Sir Richard has finished.

(seeing Mawbray applauding)

Well, well, what are you doing there? Is that the way one applauds?

MAWBRAY
Ah, pardon me, I was unable to resist the general enthusiasm. I was subjugated by reasoning so elegant—what talent—what energy.

USHER
He's a man who for three years now has done us a lot of injury.

(The usher goes to the back and looks through a side door.)

MAWBRAY
Poor Jenny—that she couldn't be here. Perhaps she would have forgotten her sorrows for a few moments—for the pleasure of vanity is not assuaged for long by the wounds of the heart. I must speak to Richard—

(The Usher returns on to the stage.)

USHER
They're coming this way.

MAWBRAY
I'll retire.

(giving him a bit of money) And renew my thanks to you.

USHER
Go through this corridor.

(He escorts him and watches him leave)

Just in time.

(Da Silva enters with Thompson.)

THOMPSON
(stopping with affected hesitation) Without being noticed, we've left the conference hall. If the Honorable Sir Richard has need of me.

DA SILVA
So be it.

(to Usher) Open those curtains and leave us.

(The Usher obeys and retires. They sit before the balustrade of the porter's room and the conversation continues.)

THOMPSON
Why, yes—the Assembly is a big distracted—one of yours has the floor.

DA SILVA
(after having listened) All that is very correct.

(Tumult in the Chamber.)

THOMPSON
Not everyone is of your opinion.

(The Speaker can be seen trying to restore order—in a voice heard over the tumult—"the First Lord of the Treasury has the floor.")

RICHARD
(in the Chamber) And as for me, I demand the floor in advance to refute what the Minster will say.

DA SILVA
(rising suddenly) He has no way of keeping it.

THOMPSON
(closing the curtains) Take care, Marquis—you will be seen.

DA SILVA
This is a war to the death.

THOMPSON
I told you that—who isn't for him is against him—and who is not for him succumbs.

DA SILVA
Let's place our cards on the table Mr. Thompson.

THOMPSON
Willingly, since you are placing all the bets.

DA SILVA
I don't want to lose my fortune. The Minister wants to remain—and the King wishes to protect the Minister chosen from the highest aristocracy.

THOMPSON
I understand the desire—but the power—?

DA SILVA
We shall have all that once Sir Richard lends us his support.

THOMPSON
You've come much too late.

DA SILVA
A meeting could repair all that.

THOMPSON
With whom?

DA SILVA
With Sir Richard.

THOMPSON
And you think you can buy and sell a conscience? You are mistaken, Marquis. You would be unsuccessful with a corruptible man—and Sir Richard has yet to be corrupted.

DA SILVA
But can't this affair be resolved through your mediation, Mr. Thompson?

THOMPSON
Whatever confidence Sir Richard has in me—still I think the thing is impossible in this way.

DA SILVA
What can be done then?

THOMPSON
Suppose Sir Richard was hidden somewhere unaware that you knew of his presence, as if you were speaking to me alone raising your voice and acquainting me with the sort of advantages Sir Richard would discover by leaving the party he has embraced. If these offers don't appear to Sir Richard in harmony with the sacrifice, he'll retire, giving me a sign with his head—his constituents cannot even reproach him with having had a meeting with a defender of the powerful—If on the contrary, the offers are agreeable to him—another sign of his head will suffice—all will take place in silence—and when it is finally agreed, he already holds—in a manner none can reproach him for, the compensation for what he has lost.

DA SILVA
That's feasible.

THOMPSON
Sooner today than tomorrow.

DA SILVA
The way must be found to put it in operation this very day!!

THOMPSON
Where?

DA SILVA
(opening the door) Would this office—

THOMPSON
A simple divides separates it.

DA SILVA
He will hear everything.

THOMPSON
And you will offer everything?

DA SILVA
Yes.

THOMPSON
And not a word which will make it known you know of his presence?

DA SILVA
I will be on my guard.

THOMPSON
Permit me to call the usher.(he calls, the Usher enters)

DA SILVA
Do it—

THOMPSON
(writing some lines with a pencil, to Usher) Go give this letter to Sir Richard.

DA SILVA
He's going to come?

THOMPSON
In an instant.

DA SILVA
Mr. Thompson— In this packet there are 100,000 pounds sterling— in exchange for good news, I shall have the honor of offering you a second which contains 800,000.

THOMPSON
Marquis—my interests are closely tied to those of Sir Richard that I can only employ what influence I have over him to decide him.

(Da Silva leaves.)

THOMPSON
For three years everything has been done for glory, for Richard's vanity. Today my reward begins.

(going to curtain, which he partially opens) They've given him my letter—he's reading it—he's coming.

(coming forward) Master, you can come.

The servant who has given himself entirely to you is commencing in the fulfillment of his promises to begin gathering up the small crumbs off your fortune.

(as Richard enters) I had you called.

RICHARD
Why? Some message from my wife, doubtless.

THOMPSON
Why do you think that?

RICHARD
On the way here, I saw Mawbray's face at the end of a corridor.

THOMPSON
I think you are mistaken.

RICHARD
In that case, what do you want?

THOMPSON
An overture from the Ministry.

RICHARD
Are the proud humiliating themselves?

THOMPSON
They are at your feet.

RICHARD
It's too late.

THOMPSON
Why's that?

RICHARD
Tomorrow the bill will be refused.

THOMPSON
Well—

RICHARD
The day after tomorrow the Ministry will fall.

THOMPSON
What will become of you?

RICHARD
Nothing.

THOMPSON
The King is too protective of the aristocracy to choose a new minister from the opposition in the House of Commons.

RICHARD
I know it.

THOMPSON
You have no opportunity then?

RICHARD
None.

THOMPSON
Whereas if the Ministry remains—

RICHARD
Well?

THOMPSON
I've already told you—it's at your feet.

RICHARD
I won't support it.

THOMPSON
You are wrong.

RICHARD
And my mandate?

THOMPSON
What about your ambition?

RICHARD
I've arrived at my goal.

THOMPSON
I think you aren't even half the way there.

RICHARD
I've considered.

THOMPSON
And your position?

RICHARD
It seems glorious to me—I've gotten this through my talent.

THOMPSON
And you'll be sustained there by your fortune. Two years stay in London have already squeezed your ten thousand pounds sterling— The death of the Doctor—then that of his wife came to support with a reasonable inheritance, the luxury you are forced to expend. Today your finest diamond is your signature on letters of credit drawn on your banker.— The retreat in which Mistress Richard lives, permits you, I know, to concentrate all your resources on a single point— But those resources are not inexhaustible— You still have three years to sit on the benches of the Chamber and they won't lead you anywhere? What will remain to you then?

RICHARD
An honorable poverty.

THOMPSON
Which will keep you from the chance of being reelected.

RICHARD
The people won't forget their champion.

THOMPSON
Your triumph intoxicates you, Richard; The people, they can only throw you down. The people are a force of nature—their rage can terrify a ministry, I conceive that the people's favor cannot reassure someone who is ambitious— Gold, positions—are they in the hands of the people? Can they dispose of it without the approval of a ministry? The people! Were you to die defending them they don't even have the right to give you a stone coffin in Westminster Abbey— Let's talk frankly, Richard.

RICHARD
Briefly—who came to you?

THOMPSON
Da Silva.

RICHARD
That Portuguese banker?

THOMPSON
Yes.

RICHARD
What interest does he take in the ministry?

THOMPSON
He's loaned the Minister considerable sums.

RICHARD
Which he fears losing—

THOMPSON
If the Ministry falls—

RICHARD
And does he come in the minister's name?

THOMPSON
To propose a treaty of peace.

RICHARD
His conditions?

THOMPSON
You shall hear them from his own mouth.

RICHARD
You let him entertain the hope that I would even consent to a discussion—naive!

THOMPSON
I would deserve that name, Richard, if I'd done what you say.

RICHARD
Then how have you arranged this?

THOMPSON
In a way that you cannot be compromised.

RICHARD
Let's see.

THOMPSON
The propositions will be made to me.

RICHARD
Where?

THOMPSON
Here.

RICHARD
And I will be?

THOMPSON
(opening the partition to the Cabinet) There—

RICHARD
Without his knowing it—

THOMPSON
That goes without saying.

RICHARD
Not bad. And Da Silva?

THOMPSON
Going to return.

RICHARD
He's just left you.

THOMPSON
At the moment I sent you that letter.

RICHARD
And be sure not a word can compromise me— Don't advance anything in my name— Let me be free to refuse everything— To disown the whole thing to deny everything.

(Richard heads toward the cabinet. Thompson opens the door to call the usher—Mawbray presents himself to him.)

THOMPSON
Assuredly—Mr. Mawbray!

RICHARD
(stopping) Mawbray!

MAWBRAY
Why does my presence seem to embarrass you so, Richard?

RICHARD
You are mistaken, Mr. Mawbray.

MAWBRAY
Perhaps it ought to, considering the motive which brings me to London; I was going wait for you at home, but having learned that you were in the House, I wanted to hear you, and I heard you.

RICHARD
(going to him) Well?

MAWBRAY
Do you know there is nothing finer than an incorruptible member, who, elected by the nation, defends it like a child would defend his mother, whose voice is always ready to condemn power, if power attempts something against the interests of the people—or its honor—who uses his private fortune as the fortune of all, and when the session is over, leaves the Chamber poor and naked like a wrestler leaving the arena! The people, Richard—the people have neither gold nor employment to give—but they decorate the altars and place their gods there.

RICHARD
That glory is beautiful, isn't it?

MAWBRAY
That glory is yours—it's what your good genius promised—what I never dared dream of for you—that today would have rewarded the virtuous Grey for adopting you—For he would have been able to say—as he died, "I have given my country a great citizen."

(While Richard listens to Mawbray with attention and pleasure, Thompson approaches Richard and says to him a low voice.)

THOMPSON
He's waiting.

RICHARD
Let him wait.

MAWBRAY
Yes, Richard—in the name of all those who love you—and who you loved, I declare that as a public man, you have exceeded all their hopes— But you've deceived them as a son, as a husband.

RICHARD
Why?

MAWBRAY
You've forgotten the prayers of your adoptive father, of his wife, when they gave you their daughter—when they said to you—"Make our Jenny happy!"

RICHARD
Don't take circumstances as a crime of my heart.

MAWBRAY
We are no longer in times when talents dispense with virtues, and glory agrees very well with goodness.

RICHARD
There's bitterness in your praise.

MAWBRAY
It's because I'm coming to speak to you in the name of a suffering wife, of a wife, you have relegated to a place far from you—to an obscure country place, and who for three months, moans over your absence with no other consoler than an old man, meaning myself, who weeps with her.

RICHARD
And why so many tears?

MAWBRAY
Because she loves you, because you disdain her.

RICHARD
Can she believe that?

MAWBRAY
She believes it, and yet she is unaware of a cruel affront.

RICHARD
What do you mean?

MAWBRAY
At your home, when I presented myself, the servants—in their replies, made me see that you are hiding your marriage here—And to spare you the blame of your valets, I had to—by shameful runarounds, explain my first words—and to associate myself in your life.

RICHARD
(to Thompson) Didn't you tell me he was waiting for me?

THOMPSON
For a long while.

MAWBRAY
I irritate you, Richard?

RICHARD
I am obliged to go in—important business.

THOMPSON
(speaking to an usher) Inform the Marquis.

MAWBRAY
Don't forget that Jenny is waiting with the greatest unease—the decision of her husband. When can we continue this conversation?

RICHARD
Why soon.

(goes into the cabinet)

MAWBRAY
How cold!

DA SILVA
(entering) Well, Mr. Thomson?

(He stops seeing Mawbray whose glance is fixed on him—Thompson observes them with astonishment and curiosity. A moment of silence.)

MAWBRAY
(pulling Thompson to him) Who is this person?

THOMPSON
The Marquis Da Silva.

MAWBRAY
Da Silva!

(THOMPSON examines Mawbray's features which display terror. Da Silva calls him aside.)

DA SILVA
Who's that man?

THOMPSON
Mawbray.

MAWBRAY
(pulling himself together) There's a curse on me here. Let's get out of here.

(he rushes out)

DA SILVA
(who has reflected) Mawbray! I don't know him.

THOMPSON
Finally, he's gone.

DA SILVA
(low) Sir Richard.

THOMPSON
(low) He's there—

DA SILVA
If you could grant me some moments, Mr. Thompson—-we will continue the conversation we were forced to interrupt.

THOMPSON
I am listening to you.

DA SILVA
I wanted to tell you.

THOMPSON
(pulling chairs near to Richard's cabinet) Sit down first.

DA SILVA
Thanks—I wanted to tell you, that at the last meeting of the Cabinet of Ministers, their Excellencies were astonished by the animosity with which Sir Richard pursued their acts. They regretted that your Master wasted the good years of his life, the passion of his eloquence, for constituents who cannot understand the sacrifices he has made for them nor appreciate the talent he wastes.

THOMPSON
You agree at least that they profit by it, and that's Sir Richard's principal aim.

DA SILVA
But what are the rewards which the people depose, Mr. Thompson?—crowns of oak, which weather suffers to tarnish into grass.

THOMPSON
And do you think that the people with a thousand voices, don't have their own ability to publicize, too? If they cannot reward, they can at least tarnish—And what you propose—for these are propositions, Marquis—will be eternal dishonor for Sir Richard—to sell himself—

DA SILVA
Yes, if it were a sale.

THOMPSON
What is it then?

DA SILVA
An alliance.

THOMPSON
An M.P. doesn't ally himself with an enemy of the people.

DA SILVA
No—but he could marry the daughter of a noble.

THOMPSON
(surprised) Marry—

DA SILVA
Sir Richard is a bachelor?

THOMPSON
(embarrassed for a moment) Yes, Marquis.

DA SILVA
His interests then change naturally. Who blames a lord for having different view than the simply deputy of the Commons? The interest of the nation, seen from his new position, presents itself to him with a new face! And point of view—low or high, creates a great difference in perspective.

THOMPSON
I admit, sir, that this changes the question.

DA SILVA
And if to a great fortune, the fiancée joined great beauty, Sir Richard is not the man to have a heart as disinterested as his conscience.

THOMPSON
But why a marriage?

DA SILVA
Because the bonds which attach us to Sir Richard must be durable.

THOMPSON
Is it an indiscretion to ask you the name?

DA SILVA
Miss Wilmer.

THOMPSON
The granddaughter of your Lordship.

DA SILVA
Yes, the child Lord Wilmer had a first marriage and my only child Caroline, adopted her when she married him. I am giving her 100,000 pounds sterling for a dowry—

THOMPSON
That's all, Marquis.

DA SILVA
Lord Wilmer was a peer of England.

THOMPSON
I know it.

DA SILVA
Perhaps it could be obtained from His Majesty to revive that title in favor of the husband of his daughter.

THOMPSON
And all three—?

DA SILVA
Will be guaranteed in the marriage contract.

THOMPSON
These are fine promises, but what guarantees Sir Richard that—?

DA SILVA
The need we have of him—

THOMPSON
Once he renounces the fight against the Bill?

DA SILVA
Then he will have the title in his hands.

THOMPSON
That's appropriate.

DA SILVA
(rising) Then you promise me—?

THOMPSON
That your offers will be faithfully reported.

DA SILVA
I place important interests in your hands, Mr. Thompson.

THOMPSON
I appreciate them.

DA SILVA
You know that time presses us— After tomorrow it will be too late—

THOMPSON
I won't forget it.

DA SILVA
Au revoir.

(Exit Da Silva.)

RICHARD
(low opening to Sir Richard) Annoying that it can only be a joke.

THOMPSON
Why's that?

RICHARD
What about my marriage?

THOMPSON
What about divorce?

RICHARD
(resting his hand on his shoulder) Repeat!

THOMPSON
Well—what's so astonishing about that? Yes—divorce.

RICHARD
And what can I reproach Jenny for that will give me grounds to obtain it?

THOMPSON
Isn't their mutual consent?

RICHARD
She will refuse—

THOMPSON
You'll force her.

RICHARD
The means—?

THOMPSON
We'll find them.

RICHARD
And when do they want a reply?

THOMPSON
By tomorrow night.

RICHARD
We'll have to hurry.

THOMPSON
Profit by Mr. Mawbray's stay in London—which leaves your wife without support, without advice.

RICHARD
Wait a minute.

(He goes to a table to write)

(Mawbray appears.)

MAWBRAY
(aside) I saw that man leave.

THOMPSON
(in a low voice to Richard) Mawbray again.

RICHARD
(continuing to write) What's it matter—?

MAWBRAY
I wanted to see you again, Richard—what might I tell Jenny?

RICHARD
My dear Mawbray—wait until tomorrow evening—I need this delay.

RICHARD
You insist on it?

RICHARD
I beg you.

(to Thompson) We will leave in an hour.

(he leaves)

MAWBRAY
(who has overheard Richard's last words) What's he say? He's leaving—a vague fear grips my heart.

(Da Silva comes in precipitously and goes to open the curtain.)

SPEAKER
(in the chamber) The floor is Sir Richard's to respond to the Finance Minister.

(Tumult in the chamber)

CONFUSED VOICES)
The floor is Sir Richard! Silence—listen!

DA SILVA
What's he going to say—?

RICHARD
(in the Chamber) I renounce the floor.

DA SILVA
The first step is taken.

THOMPSON
That doesn't cost him.

(Da Silva and Thompson leave.)

MAWBRAY
(alone) Virtuous, Anna Grey—did you alone know Richard?

CURTAIN

ACT II

Scene 4

Jenny's room in an isolated house in the country. Jenny appears on a balcony. All that can be seen are the tree tops and one must sense an immense space beneath it.

JENNY
(alone) Yet one more day spent waiting vainly by this window— counting the waves of the stream rushing into gulf—just like the hours of my life! O Richard! Richard! If my poor mother was here at least— Oh, the heart of a mother! That's where the gift of double vision takes refuge. She alone foresaw my isolation, my abandonment—she understood Richard. It's been a year since I've lived in this retreat, and Mawbray has replaced my parents— No one knows I exist, and I could die here— Surely my death would remain as hidden as my existence. Oh, but it's horrible to live like this. Since Mawbray left it seems to me that he too will never return. He promised to write to me as soon as he arrived.

(She rings and the chambermaid comes.)

JENNY
Has a letter arrived for me?

BETTY
No, Madame.

JENNY
If one should arrive you'll bring it up immediately— (hearing something) Listen—

BETTY
What?

JENNY
It's the noise—

BETTY
(listening)—of a carriage.

JENNY
A carriage, a carriage coming from that direction—oh! Let it stop! It's stopping. Betty!

BETTY
Perhaps Mr. Mawbray is returning—

JENNY
No, no—Mawbray would return by the coach to the village, from there—on foot—Go down. Go down—oh! Sir Richard alone can be coming here in a carriage. Go on then—my knees are trembling—my poor heart—

(She sits—head in her hands)

Oh, I don't dare look—from fear of seeing another person enter—But it's crazy for me to think that he's coming—this cannot be him—Madness to hope that it's him—they're coming up—it's his step—it's my Richard.

(She runs to put her arms around him as he enters)

RICHARD
What's the matter with you, Jenny?

JENNY
What's wrong? He asks me what's wrong! I've been weeping—I've been hoping forever—I've been expecting you always—even though it's a year since I've seen you—do you understand? A year—a year? And now you are here, here—my Richard—that's what's wrong with me!

RICHARD
Jenny—get hold of yourself.

JENNY
And I was accusing you, I thought you had forgotten me. I was unjust—forgive me—! You don't know? How to dare to tell you now—! By seeing me weak, uneasy because you hadn't written me—bad boy—it's three months since I received news of you—well, what was I saying? I've lost my head! Kiss me! Kiss me.

RICHARD
Perhaps you wanted me to speak with Mawbray?

JENNY
Oh, yes—forgive me, but I sent him to London.

RICHARD
I saw him.

JENNY
And why hasn't he returned with you?

RICHARD
He was tired and unable to leave until tomorrow.

JENNY
And you, when you knew of my uneasiness—tomorrow seemed too long for you—you thought you couldn't be too soon consoling your poor weeping wife— Oh, you are still my Richard—the Richard of my heart! And you left everything.

RICHARD
I wanted to talk to you without witnesses.

JENNY
Without witnesses.

RICHARD
Yes.

JENNY
Do you have some secret to tell me?

RICHARD
I have a sacrifice to ask of you.

JENNY
Of me, Richard? Oh, I am so happy! I am going to do something for you! My consent will be necessary to sell one of our farms? You must need money, your position necessitates so many expenditures.

RICHARD
It's not that.

JENNY
What is it then? But sit down, my friend.

RICHARD
It's not worth the trouble.

JENNY
Why?

RICHARD
I'm leaving in a hour.

JENNY
Without me?

RICHARD
I cannot take you.

JENNY
Well, I will still have seen you for an hour—but sit down.

RICHARD
Are you really bored here?

JENNY
I'm bored away form you. I am never bored with you. It's not my seclusion which weighs on me, it's you absence. If you would at least answer my letters—

RICHARD
You must really think—

JENNY
Oh, don't excuse yourself—I wrote too often— Often it's our demands which cool you to us women. Our life is completely taken up

with love—yours divided into twenty different passions— We ought to know it—especially me, who had news of you each day.

(pointing to newspapers) For the papers spoke to me of you— When I saw the columns interspersed with their words— "Hear, hear—bravo", I said to myself, "It's he who speaks—oh, if I were there to share in his triumph! Oh, I would be so very happy!"

RICHARD
You know of all the privations our small fortune imposes on us, living separately is, perhaps, the most necessary.

JENNY
I am submitting to it, and if I've wept, I've taken care at least that my letters to you bear no trace of my tears.

RICHARD
They would have done nothing to change our situation and would only make the two of us unhappy.

JENNY
The only thing you feared was being embarrassed by them—especially the expense of the house you'd be obliged to maintain if I were near you?

RICHARD
Indeed, that's the main thing.

JENNY
Well, cease to fear it. Of the rights my title as your wife gives me I demand only one—that of living with you—in solitude. I've little taste for the world, Richard, but I've lost my parents who loved me, and I've retained the need to be loved. Well, alone you shall go into society, where I cut a poor figure—Withdrawn in my apartment, I will see you, at least, in the evening, for a moment, or if I don't see you, I will know that you are there, near me. Ah, do you want that? No one will know I am your wife—no one will see me; no one will invite me.

RICHARD
You are mad.

JENNY
Let's speak of something else then. You've come to ask me to make a sacrifice, you said?

RICHARD
Far from keeping me from my end, this conversation is leading us there.

JENNY
Let's see.

RICHARD
New circumstances which attach to the political luck that I'm having made my position change party engagements and render again our separation very incomplete.

JENNY
Do fifteen leagues appear to you to be such a considerable distance? For the last two years haven't I been totally estranged from you? The public voice alone brings me news of you—and I was instructed at the same time as all the rest of England what my husband was doing.

RICHARD
Reproaches?

JENNY
Tears.

RICHARD
Both I find insupportable.

JENNY
But in the name of heaven—what do you want? Must I leave England the place where I was born, the land where my parents are buried? Well, I consent to it—one more day to weep over their tomb and tomorrow I will leave. But at least Richard, tell me how long this exile will last? Oh, tell me! For only one word will be the hope of all my life, "Return".

RICHARD
You are mistaken, Jenny. I have no intention of tearing you from your native land, I have not the right to doom you to abandonment.

Fate made an error binding us to each other. There's nothing for you to expiate. Can I condemn you to bear the chains of a marriage which doesn't make you a wife and will not make you a mother?

If fate, against which I've struggled for a long time separates us—I don't wish to be, I ought not to be, an eternal obstacle to your happiness and I shall have no rest, Jenny, until I've rendered you your liberty and the likelihood of having a happier future.

JENNY
I hear you without understanding you, Richard.

RICHARD
Anyway, what I propose to you almost exists—for us—with all its wrongs—and without it you could enjoy the wealth which would return to you.

JENNY
Speak, keep talking so I can understand you—or rather—shut up—for I am beginning to understand you and it's horrible.

RICHARD
While a situation—

JENNY
A word—again—

RICHARD
Legal—

JENNY
Divorce?

RICHARD
Divorce.

JENNY
Oh! My God!

RICHARD
Would reconcile everything—

JENNY

Have pity on me!

RICHARD
The word terrifies you—because you only see it surrounded by scandalous trials—shameful revelations.

JENNY
I didn't see the weapon. I felt the blow.

RICHARD
Time will cure it—you are young, Jenny, and another love—

JENNY
Oh—another love—profanation! Sacrilege! Another love! Kill me and don't insult me. Blood, but not shame.

RICHARD
There's neither blood nor shame—neither grand words nor grand gestures will divert me from my goal.

JENNY
It's atrocious—a marriage asked for by you, blessed by my father and my mother—an engagement undertaken in the face of God—and you want to break all that? The support for which they counted on for me as they died—you take it away— Finally, you ask a court to break what was bound before an altar.

RICHARD
You don't understand! A trial! Who said anything about a trial! Could I do it by myself?

JENNY
But what do you want then? Explain yourself clearly—for while I sometimes understand too much, sometimes it's not enough.

RICHARD
For you and for me—mutual consent is much better.

JENNY
You think I'm really a coward! That I would go before a judge without being dragged by the hair—to declare with my own voice, to sign with my own hand—that I am not worthy of being the wife of Sir Richard? You don't know me! You think I am only good for the tribulations of a disdained household— You think I am wiped out by your absence, You think I will bend because you will place your

arm on me—In the time of my happiness, yes—that could have been—but my tears have tempered my heart, my insomniac nights have hardened my courage, misfortunes still have made me willful— What I am, what I owe you, Richard is your own fault you can blame only yourself. Now, as to who will have the most courage, the most weakness on the greatest strength— Sir Richard I won't have it—

RICHARD
Madame, up to now, I have only uttered words of conciliation.

JENNY
Try having recourse to others.

RICHARD
(marching toward her) Jenny!

JENNY
(coldly) Richard!

RICHARD
Wretch! Do you know what I am capable of?

JENNY
I can guess.

RICHARD
And you don't tremble?

JENNY
(smiling) Look.

RICHARD
(taking her hand) Woman.

JENNY
(falling to her knees from shock) Ah!

RICHARD
On your knees!

JENNY
(raising her hands to heaven) My God have pity on me!

(she rises)

RICHARD
Oh, he'll have pity on you—for I'm going—Goodbye, Jenny, ask heaven that it be forever.

JENNY
(running to Richard and throwing her arms around his neck) Richard! Richard! Don't go!

RICHARD
Let me leave.

JENNY
If you knew how I love you.

RICHARD
Prove it to me!

JENNY
Mother! Mother!

RICHARD
Will you?

JENNY
You've really said it.

RICHARD
One more word.

JENNY
(putting her hand on his mouth) Don't say it.

RICHARD
Do you consent?

JENNY
Listen to me.

RICHARD

Do you consent? That's fine—but no more messages, no more letters—let nothing reminding me of you—let me not even know that you exist—I leave you a youth without a husband—old age without children.

JENNY
No curses—

RICHARD
Goodbye.

JENNY
You shan't go.

RICHARD
Damnation.

JENNY
Better you kill me.

RICHARD
(pushing her away) Ah—leave me alone.

JENNY
(falls, hitting her head against a corner of the furniture) Ah!

(gets up all bloody) Ah! Richard.

(She totters, holds out her arms toward her side and falls) I have to love you a lot—

(faints)

RICHARD
Fainted—injured! Blood—curses! Jenny! Jenny!

(he stanches it with his handkerchief) I don't want to remain here forever—

(comes back to her) Jenny—let's end this—! I'm retiring—you don't want to reply—goodbye then—

(starts to leave and hears a noise of steps at the door) Who is it?

THOMPSON
(appearing) From the carriage where I was keeping lookout, I just saw Mawbray leave the village coming this way.

RICHARD
What's he coming here to do?

THOMPSON
To defend his protégé—but he'll arrive too late, won't he? What have you obtained?

RICHARD
(pointing to Jenny, fainted) Nothing, despite my prayers, despite my violence—Mawbray—he's going to see her this way—new weapons against me—Jenny! Jenny! Let's forget everything!

JENNY
(coming to) Richard—me in your arms! Am I dead, am I in heaven?

RICHARD
My friend, let's forget everything.

JENNY
I don't remember anything.

(putting her hand to her face) I'm bleeding.

RICHARD
(aside) Damnation!

(aloud) Jenny—someone's coming here; dry those tears—don't let those tears of blood be seen, I beg you.

JENNY
Someone's coming, you say—who?

RICHARD
It's Mawbray!

JENNY
(sweetly) Ah, so much the better—

RICHARD
Jenny—Mawbray mustn't know of this deadly discussion—Promise me to be quiet, promise me that, I beg you—

THOMPSON
(coming to Richard) Mawbray.

RICHARD
(to Jenny) I order you!

(Mawbray enters excitedly, a moment of silence. He looks uneasily from Jenny to Richard.)

RICHARD
You here, Mawbray.

MAWBRAY
Having learned of your departure, I feared for Jenny the boredom of solitude and I hastened to return to be near her.

RICHARD
You did well, I thank you.

MAWBRAY
Should I return tomorrow to London to obtain your reply?

RICHARD
It seems to me my presence in these parts relieves you of that.

MAWBRAY
Then you've brought your wife words of consolation?

(Jenny throws herself in Richard's arms.)

RICHARD
Yes.

MAWBRAY
But only near you—that the past for her will be without sadness—and the future without anxiety.

RICHARD
Eh! Who told you she'll remain far from me?

MAWBRAY
She'll go to London?

JENNY
(seizing Richard's hands with love) Will it be true?

RICHARD
Doubtless, if you wish it so much—goodbye—I've got to go—

JENNY
Without waiting for me?

RICHARD
I can't—have to be at Parliament for the opening of the session.

(aside) The Ministers will pay me dear for the role I'm playing here.

MAWBRAY
Goodbye then.

JENNY
(to Richard) Soon.

RICHARD
Soon.

JENNY
(to Mawbray after Richard has left) My friend, I still hope to be happy.

MAWBRAY
(wiping her face) Dry this blood, Jenny—perhaps afterwards I will hope with you.

(Jenny returns to the window and sends goodbyes to Richard. Mawbray watches her with tenderness.)

CURTAIN

ACT II

Scene 5

The Council Chamber.

The Ministers of Interior and War. Two other Ministers—an usher.

MINISTER OF THE INTERIOR
Gentlemen, the Cabinet is assembled.

MINISTER OF WAR
Where is our president?

MINISTER OF THE INTERIOR
The First Lord of the Treasury is with His Majesty.

(pointing to a door at the back)

MINISTER OF WAR
Do you know what new incident caused this extraordinary meeting?

MINISTER OF THE INTERIOR
I'm unaware—but on the eve of the rejection of the bill which entails our fall, I conceive our communications must be very frequent.

USHER
(announcing) The First Lord of the Treasury.

MINISTER OF WAR
We are going to know everything, for here is our president.

FIRST LORD OF THE TREASURY

(to Usher) Leave us alone.

MINISTER OF WAR
(to first Lord) You're coming from the King?

FIRST LORD OF THE TREASURY
Yes, gentlemen.

MINISTER OF WAR
Well?

FIRST LORD OF THE TREASURY
His Majesty is more than ever leagued against the opposition which manifests itself in the House of Commons—and has put in our hands all the means in his power for us to combat it.

MINISTER OF WAR
In such circumstances as these, we must indeed confess—there is only one course left to us.

MINISTER OF THE INTERIOR
What is it?

MINISTER OF WAR
At whatever it may cost us, to bring over Sir Richard to us.

FIRST LORD OF THE TREASURY
It's to discuss him with you, gentlemen, that I've assembled you. A first overture has been made—but before going any further, I must remember we are confederates and to consult you on what remains for me to do.

MINISTER OF WAR
We are listening, Your Grace.

FIRST LORD OF THE TREASURY
Some overtures have been made by the Marquis De Silva to his secretary, Thompson—they've been received in a manner that allows us to hope for much. I thought then that such negotiations like these would be hurried—and I asked Sir Richard for a secret meeting tonight.

MINISTER OF THE INTERIOR

We presume indeed what must be their object—but to what degree can we engage ourselves?

FIRST LORD OF THE TREASURY
Gentlemen, all my promises will be realized, I have been assured, and I am authorized to promise much.

MINISTER OF WAR
But what if he resists?

FIRST LORD OF THE TREASURY
In that case, there still remains a way to try—a dangerous attempt,—unusual—a dangerous tête-à-tête.

USHER
(entering) A member of the House of Commons is asking to be introduced to Your Excellencies.

MINISTER OF WAR
His name.

USHER
The Honorable Sir Richard Darlington.

MINISTERS
Sir Richard.

FIRST LORD OF THE TREASURY
Already, in full meeting! That wasn't our agreement.

(to Usher) Have him in.

(to Ministers) We cannot dispense with receiving him.

RICHARD
Greetings to Your Excellencies.

FIRST LORD OF THE TREASURY
Be welcome, Sir Richard.

RICHARD
Is Your Grace saying what he thinks?

FIRST LORD OF THE TREASURY
A meeting was never more desired.

RICHARD
You were counting on it?

FIRST LORD OF THE TREASURY
We were hoping for it.

RICHARD
That hope is no praise for the modesty you show.

FIRST LORD OF THE TREASURY
And why's that?

RICHARD
It's that I myself still suspect this may be a dream. Me, an obscure attorney from a small village, a simple member of the House of Commons face to face with those whose names, whose political position place them around the steps of Old England's throne— It's much too bold for me, Richard Darlington, representative of the people.

FIRST LORD OF THE TREASURY
Sir, the people wrote with the blood of revolution the letters of nobility which allows them just like the old aristocracy to treat with royalty as an equal.

RICHARD
Mr. Minister, its rights are more ancient than you think—its blood banner goes back to Cromwell and it takes for speaking insignia, a crown lying on the ground beneath an axe and by a chopping block

FIRST LORD OF THE TREASURY
Is this a threat, Sir Richard?

RICHARD
It's history, sir—

FIRST LORD OF THE TREASURY
Well, Sir Richard, it's to avoid these great catastrophes between royalty and the people, whose blood is always lost in proportions little equal, that an intermediate power has been created like a double

shield which comes to lessen the pride of one and the demands of the other. Their hands, which we hold in each of ours, allow us to reunite them.

RICHARD
That cannot be done by itself, Excellency.

FIRST LORD OF THE TREASURY
Sir Richard, this is not what we were promised.

RICHARD
Promised! And who had sufficient audacity to promise in another name than his own?

FIRST LORD OF THE TREASURY
Made us hope at least.

RICHARD
A betrayal, right?

FIRST LORD OF THE TREASURY
A concession rather.

RICHARD
A concession—the people no longer make any today— They demand.

FIRST LORD OF THE TREASURY
We were able to think for a moment—

RICHARD
That I was for sale, right? It was in this hope, doubtless, that you asked me for a secret interview, but I am come to find you in the midst of your colleagues—who will hear my response and will repeat it if they so please.

FIRST LORD OF THE TREASURY
Sir, these explanations—

RICHARD
Yes, gentlemen, you came, ambassador of corruption to lay at my feet presents from the crown! Well! I repulse with my foot presents and ambassadors— All get back—

FIRST LORD OF THE TREASURY
(aside) There's only one way.

(whispers to a minister, who goes to the King's room)

RICHARD
And if tomorrow, from the height of the tribunal, I said to my constituents at what price they estimate a representative, if I denounced this infamous market of consequences, If I throw back in your face these shameful propositions?

FIRST LORD OF THE TREASURY
And what proof will you give, Sir Richard? Can't we deny it?

RICHARD
To whoever denies it I will say, "You lie!"

FIRST LORD OF THE TREASURY
Sir, we are offering you peace—you refuse— War in that case— Till tomorrow in the chamber—

RICHARD
Till tomorrow in the chamber.

(the Minister who went to the King returns and whispers in the ear of the First Lord.)

FIRST LORD OF THE TREASURY
(to Richard who is going to leave) Sir Richard, you are requested to remain a few moments in this room.

(the ministers leave.)

RICHARD
Who in the Ministry wants more of me?

USHER
(entering) There's a man who wishes to speak to you.

RICHARD
Later.

USHER
It's your secretary, I think—

RICHARD
That's good.

USHER
He seems in a great hurry to speak to you—he's waiting.

RICHARD
(impatiently) I am waiting. Why doesn't this explain itself? Is it some ruse, some snare, Let's find out what Thompson wants. The door is opening, what do I see?

UNKNOWN
Sir, you don't know me, but as for me, if I am not mistaken, you are the Secretary of the Cabinet.

RICHARD
I am, if no one else is here, Milord.

(leaning on this last word)

UNKNOWN
Very well—you've understood me.—Mr. Secretary, would you sit down at this table?

RICHARD
(still smiling) I attend Milord's orders.

UNKNOWN
(giving him some papers) Among these papers are some which demand a prompt examination. Will you indeed give me cognizance.

RICHARD
Titles of property of Count Carlston and his dependence, in Devonshire—conceded to him in perpetuity—the name is blank.

UNKNOWN
That's an omission—would you write under my dictation?

RICHARD
But—

UNKNOWN
(continuing) Richard Darlington.

RICHARD
I cannot write—

UNKNOWN
What! Mr. Secretary you refuse to write a name that I utter with the respect owed to talent?

RICHARD
This touching goodness—

UNKNOWN
You are writing, aren't you? Have the goodness to continue.

RICHARD
(reading another paper) "Letters of nobility conferring in perpetuity the title of count—"

UNKNOWN
The same names, I beg you.

RICHARD
(writing and smiling) You are obeyed.

UNKNOWN
Go on, please?

RICHARD
(reading) "A contract of marriage between Miss Lucy Wilmer, daughter of Lord Wilmer, peer of the realm, granddaughter of the Marquis De Silva and the noble Count Carlston."

UNKNOWN
We know the contracting parties—but the conditions—I beg you—

RICHARD
(reading) "The young miss brings to her husband 100,000 pounds sterling in landed property and bank shares—the Marquis De Silva, by substitution of his daughter, Caroline Wilmer, recognizes his granddaughter for his sole heir. The title of peer extinguished by the

death of Lord Wilmer, revives in the husband of his daughter and his male descendants in perpetuity."

UNKNOWN
That's all perfect—do you find that the name George, followed by the royal seal will be secured to this contract?

RICHARD
All these favors, on a single man, and in such a short while!

UNKNOWN
Ah—you are envious! Since you resist the allure so well, you must be a man of good counsel—the ministry is losing its popularity, right? The King will recoil at reconstituting it with a democratic element. He spoke recently of choosing the head of the cabinet from among the young peers—what do you think of the probable success of such a combination?

RICHARD
A devotion without bounds—

UNKNOWN
There remains one last person—

RICHARD
Blank—

UNKNOWN
You don't understand?

RICHARD
(after a moment of hesitation) So be it!

(he signs) To you this paper, Milord—these to me.

UNKNOWN
I want to tell the King we've made a deal.

RICHARD
(alone) Ah—this is a dream! A madness—! an apparition!—but, these papers—! Ah, no—all this is real—oh! I cannot breathe, my head is turning—Richard! Richard! In your most brilliant thoughts did you ever dare foresee—? Me! Me! Allied to what in England is

the most illustrious! Richard Count! Richard Peer! Richard Minister! Richard the first in the realm after the King—what do I say—? The King—the King—he's only a name—it's the minister who governs. It's the ministry that directs all finances, war, administration.

(going to the Prime Minister's seat) Here's my place—here's the throne, the real throne. From here my voice will reverberate in the three Kingdoms—over the ocean.

(striking his head) From here will emit—the will that the universe submits to. Mine the honors, the dignities, crowns—mine the armorial bearings, a banner, millions to lavish to enrich London. England with monuments, eternal monuments, on which we'll be read forever—my name, a name that I am making, that I bequeath to my country like fame. Ah, my joy—my happiness—you choke me—

(to Thompson who enters) Come—come—do you know?

THOMPSON
Sir Richard.

RICHARD
Do you know?

THOMPSON
Mawbray has returned to London.

RICHARD
Eh! What's the matter?

THOMPSON
He's bringing your wife.

RICHARD
Jenny.

THOMPSON
She's waiting for you at your hotel.

RICHARD
I'd forgotten everything. Curses!

CURTAIN

ACT III

Scene 6

An apartment in Richard's hotel in London.

JENNY
I would never dare await his return without you, Mawbray.

MAWBRAY
Without me, what do you fear?

JENNY
A sudden reaction of rage.

MAWBRAY
And since when can't a woman come to her husband's home?

JENNY
But without doubt he has motives for hiding this marriage—since no one here knows of it.

MAWBRAY
It exists nonetheless, Jenny. It is none the less sacred.

JENNY
Oh, don't speak so loud: These servants might hear you.

MAWBRAY
As it must—sooner or later be they that call you Mrs. Richard.

JENNY
Oh—you will agree, Mawbray, that Richard alone has the right to give them that order.

MAWBRAY
Listen.

JENNY
Someone's coming—it's him! Mawbray let me go. I don't want, I don't dare see him—it's you, Mawbray who dragged me here. I was wrong. Oh! Hide me—in the name of heaven, hide me!

MAWBRAY
(to a servant) As I must speak to Sir Richard alone, escort Madame into another room.

JENNY
Be calm, Mawbray, manage his pride—

MAWBRAY
Yes—up until we force it to bend. Don't worry.

(Jenny leaves. Mawbray looks in the antechamber.)

MAWBRAY
It's him—a woman!

SERVANT
(to Lady Wilmer) The name Milord.

LADY WILMER
I desire to make it known only to Sir Richard.

MAWBRAY
What do I see?

SERVANT
Sir Richard is absent.

LADY WILMER
I will await his return.

MAWBRAY
(aside) Lady Wilmer—Caroline De Silva—and me, me here—me who she might recognize! Where can I hide—? Oh—this cabinet.

SERVANT
Will you enter this room, Milady—someone is awaiting Sir Richard there.

LADY WILMER
(entering enveloped in her veil) Someone? That servant is mistaken—so much the better.

THOMPSON
(crossing the antechamber) Sir Richard.

RICHARD
(to a Servant) A lady is waiting for me.

SERVANT
Yes, sir—

RICHARD
Where?

SERVANT
In that room.

RICHARD
Thompson, watch that no one comes to trouble us.

(entering and closing the door in a rage) By God! Madame—

LADY WILMER
(rising) Sir Richard.

RICHARD
(with respect) Pardon, Milady—but I find in this room a person I didn't think to have the honor of seeing here—and I am looking vainly for someone I expected to meet—give yourself the trouble of sitting down. I am at your orders.

LADY WILMER
Sir, I am taking steps to see you—

RICHARD
May I know first, Milady to whom I have the honor of speaking?

LADY WILMER
To Lady Wilmer.

RICHARD
(rising) Daughter of Marquis De Silva?

LADY WILMER
Herself—sit down then.

RICHARD
Allow me, Milady.

LADY WILMER
Sit down, I beg you, Sir Richard, I have things of the greatest importance to communicate to you. Are you sure that no one can hear us?

RICHARD
I am certain of it.

LADY WILMER
My father spoke to me yesterday of plans for a union to exist between our two families.

RICHARD
Yes, Milady—

LADY WILMER
The King himself intends to interest himself in the marriage of my adopted daughter.

RICHARD
I know the goodness of His Majesty.

LADY WILMER
My father, the Marquis De Silva is giving 100,000 pounds sterling—

RICHARD
These details.

LADY WILMER
Are necessary, and prepare the secret I have to reveal to you.

RICHARD
I am listening.

LADY WILMER
(taking his hand) Sir Richard!

RICHARD
Milady.

LADY WILMER
Oh, I will never dare—Sir Richard—you are an honest man?

RICHARD
Up until the present, I have never given any person the right to doubt it.

LADY WILMER
You, my father, and one other person alone will know the secret I am going to tell you.

RICHARD
Whatever this secret may be—it will die here.

LADY WILMER
Perhaps you thought, sir, that by marrying Miss Wilmer, although she was a child of my husband's first marriage—the almost maternal love that I bear her will determine me to join my personal fortune to hers.

RICHARD
Milady, perhaps I should have the right to complain of your persistence in returning to such details. If they've painted me in your eyes as an interested man—permit me to tell you that the portrait is neither flattering nor accurate.

LADY WILMER
Oh—far from that, Sir! I know all your generosity. But you don't understand that I have a secret, a humiliating secret to reveal to you and that I am delaying—?

(a pause) I have a son, Sir Richard, and my fortune belongs to him.

RICHARD
You?

LADY WILMER
Yes, the child of a sin—and three persons, you understand, alone know of the existence of the wretched child.

RICHARD
And Lord Wilmer?

LADY WILMER
He was always unaware of it. Some months after our marriage he received his commission as Governor India from which I never returned until after his death.

RICHARD
Well, Milady?

LADY WILMER
Well, hardly had I set foot on English soil reclaiming ownership over my property, than I thought of the poor abandoned one, disinherited of his mother's caresses, let him find his fortune, at least, for this child was perhaps cursed by me—as for me, me, I have always loved him like a mother, meaning with a love at all hours at all moments. My child, my son—do you believe he will pardon me?

RICHARD
Finding you again and taking you in his arms, he will forget everything.

LADY WILMER
Oh—that's what makes my unhappiness— Because I can never see him again, that I am condemned never to press him to my heart, the heart of a mother still.

RICHARD
And why's that? Pardon, Madame—but having half your secret perhaps I have the right to know the rest.

LADY WILMER
I will never see my son again.

RICHARD
Why?

LADY WILMER
He would want to know his father, his father that I cannot name, do you understand? And a son who will ask me the name of his father prevents me from telling him.

RICHARD
Yes, then you are right, better than he remain unaware.

LADY WILMER
And only my death, in receiving my fortune will he know my secret—yes—that's what I said to myself but from here to there—he may perhaps be wretched, in need, remembering and cursing his mother—oh, don't you see yet what I've come to ask of you?

RICHARD
Yes, Madame, to replace for him what he's lost, right? If he's younger than me, he will be my son—Milady, if he's my age, he will be my brother.

LADY WILMER
I wasn't mistaken! Oh, you have all the virtues, let me embrace your knees.

RICHARD
Madame.

LADY WILMER
You don't understand that a mother whose son was taken from her—for it's returning him to me—I will see him again; he won't know that I am his mother—Oh, Richard—pardon! Sir Richard, you will go yourself to discover him in Northumberland?

RICHARD
I know the country, Milady.

LADY WILMER
Have I said in what county? In Darlington.

RICHARD
Darlington!

LADY WILMER
You will inform yourself of an honest man, of his wife—who must be very old by now—of a worthy doctor—of Doctor Grey.

RICHARD
(aside) She's my mother!

LADY WILMER
And, if they are dead, if the young man, if my son has left the country, you will learn where he went, won't you—you will discover him—

RICHARD
(still aside) And who perchance is my father?

LADY WILMER
You aren't answering me.

RICHARD
A doubt troubles me, Madame, and suppose this young man were to question me—

LADY WILMER
What?

RICHARD
Yes—a fortune only constitutes half a position in society—it's the name of a father which completes it. Do you have the right, Madame, to hide this name from him? To hide it from him is a theft. Tell me the name, Madame, or failing that—

LADY WILMER
Well—?

RICHARD
Failing that, oh! It's impossible, the name of his father, but for your own sake if you want this son not to curse you. Mercy, that name—that name! But you don't have the right to hide it— Perhaps your son knows you—Perhaps he's only waiting for a word to fall at your feet—Oh! You are not his mother if you don't tell me that name—The name of the father of your child, Madame, his name.

LADY WILMER
And if I don't tell you?

RICHARD
Then Madame, your secret is sacred, I will keep it. But find someone else to go say to a wretched child, "You have a mother who doesn't wish to meet you and who sends you money in default of caresses. You have a father, he's living perhaps and he's afraid of being compromised by telling you his name." And then the son—

LADY WILMER
Well?

RICHARD
Well, the son will reply "Let my mother keep her gold, my father his secret, and curse on both of you!"

LADY WILMER
Oh, My God!

RICHARD
His name, Madame! That's the only condition—

LADY WILMER
You really want it—

RICHARD
Oh—I insist—

LADY WILMER
Well, his father—

MAWBRAY
(violently opened the door of the cabinet) Milady Wilmer—this secret belongs to someone else and you have no right to reveal it—

LADY WILMER
Heavens Roberts—

MAWBRAY
Silence.

RICHARD
What do you mean by this?

MAWBRAY
Accept my arm.

RICHARD
I won't suffer it.

MAWBRAY
Richard! It's the will of Milady.

RICHARD
Is it true, Madame.

LADY WILMER
Oh, yes, yes—let's leave—so I can hide myself from all eyes.

RICHARD
At least this conversation—

MAWBRAY
Forget this conversation, Richard.

(He leaves with Lady Wilmer.)

RICHARD
Curse on that man coming in just as I was about to learn everything.

THOMPSON
What's all this I see signify? Mawbray—that woman—

RICHARD
That woman, Thompson—she's my mother.

THOMPSON
Lady Wilmer! And your father—?

RICHARD
I was about to learn when Mawbray came out of that cabinet.

THOMPSON
He heard you?

RICHARD
That man is always around.

THOMPSON
It was he who forced you to refuse everything.

RICHARD
No—I accepted everything.

THOMPSON
Accepted?

RICHARD
All is promised.

THOMPSON
And Lady Wilmer was speaking to you about the planned….

RICHARD
Yes.

THOMPSON
And Mawbray heard you? All is lost.

RICHARD
No—because he'll never see Jenny any more. Eternal separation between her and this genie who protects her and pursues me. Here he is. Will you tell me, sir, by what right you meddle in my destiny?

MAWBRAY
That language.

RICHARD
Is that of a man justly irritated.

MAWBRAY
You are forgetting!

RICHARD
Do I know you? Do I owe you something?

MAWBRAY
You owe respect to my white hair, confidence to the friend of your adoptive father who bequeathed me a role in his paternal power.

RICHARD
He didn't intend to bequeath me a spy—a breeder of discord in my household.

MAWBRAY
Let Jenny be happy—I will lose my only right over her—that of her protector.

RICHARD
Happy or not, all right in her favor.

MAWBRAY
What are your intentions?

RICHARD
That from this moment you will never approach her again.

MAWBRAY
Do you mean to tell me you are kicking me out?

RICHARD
Take it anyway you like.

MAWBRAY
Have you though that you are speaking to an old man who, for the last fifteen years has put his whole life in you, in Jenny—whose hopes, whose thoughts, whose only prayer has been your happiness through her and her happiness through you? Richard, in speaking thus, have you thought you are killing me?

THOMPSON
Can there be anything in common between Sir Richard and a foreigner who bears a false name?

MAWBRAY
The intervention of your valet enlightens me—You have it in for Jenny and are removing the only support remaining to her.

RICHARD
Enough speculation!

MAWBRAY
Richard, I will babble the plans of this man and yours—under your roof, in the street, I will watch over her.

RICHARD
That's enough! Get out—

MAWBRAY
Wretch—you don't know that I am born to punish.

(he leaves)

RICHARD
And that will be the way of such like obstacles which stop me!

THOMPSON
It was madness to suffer it for a single hour.

RICHARD
My mother, a De Silva, of the first nobility of Portugal. Lady Wilmer of the first nobility of England—and my father—she doesn't want to name him!

THOMPSON
Perhaps, some obscure man that her father's pride prevented her—

RICHARD
And obscure man, you say? Her? No, no—his blood which beats in my heart tells me no. She whose daughter the King protects—the King—these offers, these promises, this peerage to me, mine, Richard Darlington. Oh, my head spins, my blood rises.

THOMPSON
What's wrong with you?

RICHARD
If I were touching that throne for that interview!

THOMPSON
An interview?

RICHARD
It's a secret, silence!

THOMPSON
And you promised, you say—?

RICHARD
To sign the contract of marriage this evening—

THOMPSON
Where?

RICHARD
The place hasn't been fixed.

THOMPSON
Not here, certainly—not in London.

THOMPSON
Then where?

RICHARD
The house in the country where Jenny lives.

THOMPSON
Perfect—

RICHARD
Isolated.

THOMPSON
That's true—

RICHARD
Hardly finished.

THOMPSON
The apartment your wife inhabited—

RICHARD
There can be traces of her stay there.

THOMPSON
You'll get these first and all will disappear.

RICHARD
And Jenny—what to do about her?

THOMPSON
Do you think she will continue to refuse?

RICHARD
I am sure of it.

THOMPSON
Carry her off—

RICHARD
Who'll do that.

THOMPSON
Me.

RICHARD
She'll resist.

THOMPSON
She'll think she's returning to the country.

RICHARD
Where will you take her?

THOMPSON
It's only thirty leagues from London to Dover and seven from Dover to Calais.

RICHARD
 France.

THOMPSON
Where you will send her a queen's fortune.

RICHARD
Once in France, she will accuse me.

THOMPSON
She won't dare.

RICHARD
And if she dared?

THOMPSON
Listen!

RICHARD
What?

THOMPSON
It's either God or Hell; wait—

RICHARD
Speak!

THOMPSON
After having left her in France, I will return by way of Northumberland.

RICHARD
Well—?

THOMPSON
I'll pass through Darlington.

RICHARD
And then?

THOMPSON
I know the pastor.

RICHARD
So?

THOMPSON
I'll go to him—in his house, in his records—that's where you act if marriage is to be found—the year?

RICHARD
1813.

THOMPSON
The month?

RICHARD
June.

THOMPSON
Do you understand?

RICHARD
No.

THOMPSON
The only legal document, the only one which could prove your union—

RICHARD
Well—

THOMPSON
The page—I'll tear it out, I'll bring it to you—you'll destroy it—and let Jenny come with her shouts—her tears—no proof.

RICHARD
No proof.

THOMPSON
And we are saved.

RICHARD
But are you indeed sure of succeeding?

THOMPSON
I've said it, that document will be destroyed—even if I have to burn the record—I won't ask anything of you until then—but then—

RICHARD
Then?

THOMPSON
There will be a crime between the two of us—Sir Richard.

RICHARD
I will be your protector.

THOMPSON
Oh—better than that—you will be my accomplice.

RICHARD
Accomplice—so be it! But let's hurry.

THOMPSON
What has to be done?

RICHARD
Stop by the home of the Marquis, give him a rendezvous for this evening with all the family at my country home—excuse me for preceding them there. Tell them that it is indispensable—say whatever you like.

THOMPSON
From there?

RICHARD
Run—retain post horses—you will return here, take my carriage—Jenny will be ready.

THOMPSON
You're sure of it?

RICHARD
I'll see to it.

(to a servant) Isn't there a woman waiting for me hereabouts?

SERVANT
In that room.

RICHARD
Tell her to come. You, Thompson, get going—she mustn't see you. To the Marquis De Silva—a rendezvous tonight in my home in the country—then post horses and the sea between the two of us—I was forgetting—there are five hundred pounds sterling in this wallet—you will leave them all with her that you don't need for the return. Till tonight—think about it.

(Thompson leaves.)

SERVANT
Here's that lady.

RICHARD
Fine. Lock the doors—I am not here for anyone—for anyone—do you understand?

(Servant leaves; Jenny enters.)

JENNY
Richard.

RICHARD
Come, Madame, come.

JENNY
Where is Mawbray?

RICHARD
Out of this hotel—where I hope he'll never reenter.

JENNY
You've—?

RICHARD
Kicked him out like a spy. Do you know, Madame, that I am tired of his remonstrances? I'd hardly be able to support them from someone who had the right to make them to me— That man will ruin us by placing himself between the two of us— He constantly agitates you to betray the first duty of a wife—obedience.

JENNY
Oh, my God—but that's not his way.

RICHARD
I tell you I am tired of having you always on my heels—like my shadow—That's a bad way to bring back one's husband—pursuing him with annoyances and complaints.

JENNY
But it's not him?

RICHARD
Then it's you then? You are here? Well—he tires me, and I am ridding myself of him first.

JENNY
And how it's my turn, isn't it? Oh—how cruel you are.

RICHARD
Eh! My God, Tears! If you begin that way, where will you end?

JENNY
Richard, you shan't leave me this way. Oh! Why. It's a servant that you are sending away—that you are kicking out, and not a wife. As for me, I am still your wife—before God, before men— The wife you chose yourself, that no one forced you to take—I loved you, I did—did I tell you that first? Did I seek to seduce you? Oh! No, why it was you— You came to me, remember?

RICHARD
Finally, what do you want? What are you asking of me? Who brought you here—? What did you come to do here?

JENNY
To ask you again for a bit of your old love.

RICHARD
My love! You are mad!

JENNY
Why recall the past?

RICHARD
The past—that's nothing.

JENNY
Oh—you never loved me?

RICHARD
Well—no—hear me—I had need of a family, of a social position, you were there—I could've loved another like you—I loved you like another.

JENNY
Infamous—

RICHARD
Society places around every man of genius—instruments—his to use.

JENNY
Why, that's horrible.

RICHARD
I don't love you, I never loved you.

JENNY
Shut up, shut up!

RICHARD
Judge now if you ought to stay.

JENNY
No, no, sir, I am leaving.

RICHARD
(to a servant) Horses!

JENNY
I need to go forget, far from you, the horrible nightmare of these two days. A moment will come when the head, less ardent, will hear the voice of your heart, you will remember Jenny—But before coming to implore your pardon, you'll have to ask if she's not dead.

RICHARD
(going to the window) Thompson—hitch 'em up.

JENNY
With whom shall I leave?

RICHARD
My secretary will accompany you—

JENNY
I prefer to go alone.

RICHARD
I won't allow it—understand?

JENNY
Why not with Mawbray—?

RICHARD
Do you know where he is, and do you think I want to go find him throughout the city? You will write him to come rejoin you.

JENNY
Oh—to leave us like this! To see a woman in tears, despair in the soul, praying on her knees, imploring a word, a glance—

RICHARD
Madame—they are going to wait for you—Make your last preparations—

JENNY
I obey—

(as she goes) Oh, mother, mother!

(she leaves)

(Thompson appears.)

THOMPSON
I've seen the Marquis.

RICHARD
Good, the contract?

THOMPSON
Will be signed tonight.

RICHARD
At my home?

THOMPSON
Yes.

RICHARD
And everything is ready for your departure?

THOMPSON
Everything. In eight hours, Dover, at ten at Calais—five days, here.

RICHARD
This evening, the contract signed, tomorrow the marriage—the same day—the peerage—you'll find me a minister.

THOMPSON
Your Excellency's last orders—

RICHARD
Full gallop to Dover.

(goes to the cabinet)

JENNY
(returning) Goodbye Richard—where is he?

THOMPSON
Gone.

JENNY
Gone without seeing me, without telling me goodbye—Oh, that's the last straw! Come, sir, I am ready (Jenny and Thompson leave.)

(Richard comes out slowly—follows behind them, looks out the window of the antechamber—the wheels of a carriage can be heard—the noise of the postilion's whip)

RICHARD
(drying his face) Finally!

SERVANT
Shall I accompany you, sir?

RICHARD
(returning) Yes, James, you'll come with me.

BLACKOUT

ACT III

Scene 7

A great highway.

MAWBRAY
(alone behind a tree bordering the road) It's a rape—an infamous rape— Against which I cannot invoke the law—for to invoke it, I would have to disclose myself— Against whom could I invoke it? Against my son? Oh, Richard! If you have a demon you also have your good genius.

He's a man who is dazzled, who is ruining himself, selling himself! Misfortune! So many hopes lie on his head! It's for that, it's to be free that he had me refused admittance at the door of his hotel.

Oh, thanks; Richard for I saw your faithful Thompson leave, I saw him return with post horses, I learned which road they were going to take. All my hope and that of Jenny is now in me—In me, an isolated being around whom the chains of society have been broken and who leans on no one for support— Come, old man, rediscover your heart and the hand of youth for both have never been more necessary— Is that their carriage?

No—night is beginning to fall—So much the better, this road will be more solitary. Ah, Thompson! Intriguing lieutenant, half trickster, more than half murderer—Thompson, Thompson, you have to settle with me the account of Richard's honor and Jenny's happiness! Bad luck to you, Thompson— A noise of horses—

(bending to the ground to listen) Well, so be it, let's hide ourselves like a brigand behind this tree— The role is taken Jenny. I have to help Jenny, I have to by any means possible— They are approaching— Come, let God see and judge.

(hurling himself at the head of the horses) Coachman, stop.

POSTILION
Whoa!

MAWBRAY
Don't be afraid, I am not a murderer. Aren't you taking two people?

THOMPSON
(sticking his head out) What's wrong, coachman?

MAWBRAY
It's them!

THOMPSON
Mawbray! Coachman, put her in gallop!

MAWBRAY
If you take a step, you are dead! Get down!

(The coachman leaps down by his horses)

Jenny, are you there?

THOMPSON
(in the carriage) Silence, Madame.

JENNY
(in a shocked voice) Mawbray, Mawbray.

MAWBRAY
(opening the door) Ah!

THOMPSON
(rushing out and pushing Mawbray back) What do you want?

MAWBRAY
To speak to Jenny—

THOMPSON
Impossible.

MAWBRAY
Jenny!

THOMPSON
Sir!

MAWBRAY
Oh—don't touch me—Jenny, where do you think you are going—?

THOMPSON
Silence!

JENNY
To Richard's country house.

MAWBRAY
France! You are going to France!

THOMPSON
Curse! Shut up.

MAWBRAY
Do you understand? He's kidnapping you.

JENNY
Oh!

MAWBRAY
You don't know then?

(to the coachman) Help this young woman down— Or you are the accomplice of this miserable wretch.

JENNY
My God! My God! What to do?

MAWBRAY
(reopening the carriage door) Get down.

THOMPSON
A last time.

MAWBRAY
Get down, Jenny; in the name of your dead parents, I order you—

THOMPSON
(threateningly) Sir!

JENNY
Mawbray! Mawbray, watch out!

THOMPSON
Coachman, help me.

MAWBRAY
Not a step.

THOMPSON
(pulling out a pistol) So that's what you want? Well—

(pulling Jenny aside)

Death and damnation to you—!

(fires, wounding Mawbray in the left arm)

MAWBRAY
(coldly) Your hand was trembling, coward. To you the same and the same words. Death and damnation.

(he fires on Thompson as he puts his foot on the coach step)

THOMPSON
(totters) Ah!

(falling)

MAWBRAY
Coachman, here's gold. Not an instant to lose—to horse. To sir Richard's country house.

THOMPSON
(clinging to the coach) Help me—help me— Can't you see I am dying, that I am mortally wounded—? Murderers! Demons! Oh!

(He releases the coach as it leaves—then he gets up and crawls to a tree) Help me—help me—down there—you.

(He pulls himself for a moment onto the road—then he falls dead)

BLACKOUT

ACT III

Scene 8

(Jenny's room.)

JENNY
(entering with Mawbray) You are wounded, Mawbray?

MAWBRAY
Nothing, the ball only grazed the skin.

JENNY
But what's going to become of me? For there can no longer be any doubt, he intended to rid himself of me— My presence in England troubles him— Who knows even if my life is not at risk?

MAWBRAY
Jenny, I've got one way remaining to assure your safety. I hesitated to employ it, but to hesitate any longer would almost be a crime— Jenny there's a secret between Richard and me— His ambition alone persecutes you— This secret can annihilate all his hopes— I've delayed a long while, you see, for I love him.

JENNY
And me, too!

MAWBRAY
Because I was proud of his success I hid this secret from him. It opens a gulf between him and the future—with so much mystery that if he forces me, I will advertise it publicly to teach him— Then,

Jenny, I hope he himself will withdraw from these political affairs which separate him from you— Then, Jenny, you must spare him all reproach, for he will be, in his turn, more wretched than you have ever been.

JENNY
Oh, if that's so then keep the secret, and may I alone be wretched.

MAWBRAY
Impossible, Jenny—for you don't know everything— For your fate is not all that is threatened. Richard is on the point of becoming as bad a citizen as he has been a bad husband— For the influence he's had on your destiny, he can have on the destiny of England.

JENNY
And this secret—this word you will tell him?

MAWBRAY
That word which Richard alone must hear will remain secret between him and me, will change everything Jenny, bring him to your feet, very happy to be back in your life. Jenny, you are going to remain here.

JENNY
Alone?

MAWBRAY
As I pass through the village, I will send Betty.

JENNY
And where are you going?

MAWBRAY
To London.

JENNY
To find Richard.

MAWBRAY
I have to see him before tomorrow.

JENNY
Tomorrow will be too late?

MAWBRAY
Perhaps.

JENNY
It's this night, this darkness which frightens me.

MAWBRAY
Child, what have you to fear?

JENNY
Nothing—I know it.

MAWBRAY
Haven't you lived for a year in this house?

JENNY
Yes, yes.

MAWBRAY
In an hour, Betty will be here.

JENNY
I implore your protection, don't forget it.

MAWBRAY
No—my child—goodbye.

JENNY
Goodbye, Mawbray! Goodbye, my protector, my father! Will I ever love you enough—you who love me so much? Goodbye. Lock me in— Goodbye again. Oh! God! My God!

MAWBRAY
You are weeping?

JENNY
Yes, so many things are happening to me—upsetting my life, that when a friend leaves me, I tremble that I will never see him again.

MAWBRAY
Come, my child, you will see me again and Richard with me.

(Exit Mawbray.)

JENNY
(alone) Oh, if that's the case, leave, leave quickly, my father!

(to Mawbray after he has locked the door) Goodbye. Goodbye.

(falling into an armchair) Oh, what a strange thing! Here I am as I was yesterday, and during this interval of a few hours, Richard came here, then I followed him to London, then I was dragged off by that wretch! Sometimes there are events enough for a lifetime all in the events of one day! I've hardly been able to think that all this is true! I think I am sleeping and that it is a terrible dream that is pursuing me. Oh, no, no, it's all true, all real. Oh, my God, I'm suffocating. I need some air.

(going to the balcony) How calm everything is! How peaceful! Would anyone say in the midst of this reposeful Nature that there was anyone who wakes and suffers. Oh, mother, mother! Pardon— but many's the time on this balcony, on the place where I stand, I've calculated the depth of this gulf—Many times I've thought—forgive me mother, that a poor creature who had no more strength to bear these evils—would find it in the depth of this precipice.

Oh, mother, mother, forgive me—Richard is going to return and I will be happy— And then thoughts like these will no longer come to your poor daughter.

(raising her head) But what do I see down there on the road—a carriage—It's coming this way—-and with what speed! Eh—why, its horse is running away—no—no—it's indeed coming here—it's stopping— Who can it be? A man's getting out— He's opening the door that Mawbray locked— It's Richard—Richard alone has a second key to this house. Oh, Richard, Richard, is going to see me— He believes I left for France! My God—some place to hide myself—

(runs to the door) And Mawbray locked me in here—! And I told him to do it—Misfortune, misfortune! Oh—he's here—my God! This cabinet.

(she runs into it)

RICHARD

(enters followed by a servant) I've got here in time—barely enough if I have a half hour in advance of the Marquis and his family—James, bring torches and keep by the door to escort in those persons who will present themselves at any moment. Fine. Go.

(drawing his watch) Eight o'clock—Thompson must be in Dover by now—and, by tomorrow morning he will be in Calais—God keep him! Let's see if anything here indicates this apartment was occupied by a woman.

(noticing a hat and a shawl) That precaution wasn't needless. Where to put this? I don't have the keys to these armoires. Throw them out the window where they'll be found tomorrow. Ah, lights on the top of the mountain— Doubtless it's the Marquis. He's punctual. But what the devil to do with these muslins? Ah, this closet! I'll pull back the bolt.

(opening the closet)

JENNY
Ah.

RICHARD
(seizing here by the arm) Who is there?

JENNY
Me! Me! Don't hurt me!

RICHARD
(drawing her out of the cabinet) Jenny! Why she's a demon who throws herself in my face every time I think I'm rid of her. What are you doing here? Who brought you? Speak quickly! Quickly.

JENNY
Mawbray.

RICHARD
Always Mawbray! Where is he? So I can at least avenge myself on a man!

JENNY
He's far, far off—went back to London, mercy for him!

RICHARD
Well?

JENNY
He stopped the carriage.

RICHARD
And then? Can't you see I am on fire?

JENNY
And as for me, I—

RICHARD
And then, I tell you?

JENNY
They fought.

RICHARD
And—

JENNY
And Mawbray killed Thompson.

RICHARD
Hell! And he brought you here?

JENNY
Yes! Yes, pardon—!

RICHARD
Jenny, Jenny, listen!

JENNY
It's the wheels of a carriage.

RICHARD
It's bringing me my wife and her family.

JENNY
And what about me?— What am I?

RICHARD
You Jenny, you are my evil genius. You are the abyss that swallows all my aspirations— You are the demon who will push me to the scaffold—for I will commit a crime.

JENNY
Oh, my God!

RICHARD
It's because there's no way to go back—you see. You wouldn't sign the divorce, you wouldn't leave England.

JENNY
Now, now—I want whatever you want.

RICHARD
Now, it's too late.

JENNY
What are you going to do?

RICHARD
I don't know—but pray God!

JENNY
Richard.

RICHARD
(putting his hand over her mouth) Silence! Don't you hear them? Don't you hear them? They're coming up. They're going to find a woman here.

(running to the door he locks it with a double lock)

JENNY
(running to the balcony) Help! Help!

RICHARD
They mustn't find you here, you understand.

JENNY
(on her knees) Pity! Pity!

RICHARD
I've had enough of pity.

JENNY
(trying to shout) Help me!

(A noise can be heard on the stairway. Richard locks the transept window and finds himself outside on the balcony)

JENNY
Help me!

RICHARD
Curses!

(One hears a scream repeated in the precipice. Richard reopens the window and is alone on the balcony. He comes forward, pale, drying his face, and goes to open the door.)

(Enter De Silva, Miss Wilmer, and the First Lord of the Treasury.)

DA SILVA
Pardon, you were locked in, Sir Richard—but your servant told us you were expecting us.

RICHARD
Yes, excuse me. That key—got in there itself—I didn't know it—

DA SILVA
(to a young miss) Miss Wilmer.

RICHARD
(bowing) Miss.

DA SILVA
And you ill? You are very pale?

RICHARD
You find me so? It's nothing. Everything is ready, you see.

DA SILVA
His Excellency would like to serve us a witness! Don't you have yours?

RICHARD
No—no need. Let's sign, sign.

(Da Silva has Miss Wilmer sign and presents the contract to Richard)

DA SILVA
Your hand is trembling, Sir Richard!

RICHARD
Mine! Not at all.

(He goes to sign. As he turns his notices, Mawbray, motionless and pale near him—his eyes fixed on Richard)

MAWBRAY
If you need a witness, Richard—I'm here.

RICHARD
So be it—you're as good as another.

(low) If you say a word!

DA SILVA
What's the meaning of this fellow?

MAWBRAY
(low) Richard, it's for me to threaten and not you. Listen!

RICHARD
Sir—

MAWBRAY
Speak low—

RICHARD
By what right—

MAWBRAY
Look at that balcony.

RICHARD
In your turn, silence!

MAWBRAY
I was on the highway—facing it.

RICHARD
Where?

MAWBRAY
I was there, I tell you—

RICHARD
Well?

MAWBRAY
I witnessed.

RICHARD
Well?

MAWBRAY
With a word I can—

RICHARD
You won't say it.

MAWBRAY
Why?

RICHARD
You would have already done so.

MAWBRAY
I can be silent.

RICHARD
Ah—

MAWBRAY
On one condition.

RICHARD
Which is?

MAWBRAY
Break off this marriage, abandon London renounce the House— We will retire together in some isolated corner of England wheresoever we can— You to repent, me to weep.

RICHARD
Mawbray, I told you if you were able to denounce me, you would have done so already—A reason I am unaware of prevents you—That's all I need.

MAWBRAY
Then you refuse.

RICHARD
I refuse.

MAWBRAY
Decidedly?

RICHARD
(crossing in front of him and presenting the pen to the Marquis) Now your turn, Marquis.

MAWBRAY
(holding Richard by the arm) Stop!

(to Richard) There's still time.

RICHARD
Sign!

MAWBRAY
(loudly) Marquis Da Silva.

DA SILVA
Sir?

MAWBRAY
Do you remember the village of Darlington?

DA SILVA
What?

MAWBRAY
The night you pursued a young girl who was being carried away?

DA SILVA
Silence, sir!

MAWBRAY
I won't name her—she bore a child.

DA SILVA
Well?

MAWBRAY
You only saw the father of that child for an instant, only a second—but that must be enough to recognize him forever—Marquis, look me carefully in the face.

DA SILVA
It was you.

MAWBRAY
Myself.

(pointing to Richard) Behold my son!

DA SILVA
Then you are—

MAWBRAY
The executioner.

(Richard collapses prostrated.)

CURTAIN

ABOUT FRANK J. MORLOCK

FRANK J. MORLOCK has written and translated many plays since retiring from the legal profession in 1992. His translations have also appeared on Project Gutenberg, the Alexandre Dumas Père web page, Literature in the Age of Napoléon, Infinite Artistries.com, and Munsey's (formerly Blackmask). In 2006 he received an award from the North American Jules Verne Society for his translations of Verne's plays. He lives and works in México.

www.ingramcontent.com/pod-product-compliance
Lightning Source LLC
LaVergne TN
LVHW041623070426
835507LV00008B/411